041908

HV
8290
.N53

Nielsen, Swen C.

General
organizational and
administrative
concepts for
university police

DATE		
JUL 31 1988		
APR 5 1989		
JUN 27 1994		
OCT 28 1994		
NOV 9 2005		

mill woods

© THE BAKER & TAYLOR CO.

General Organizational and
Administrative Concepts
for
University Police

General Organizational and Administrative Concepts for University Police

By

SWEN C. NIELSEN, M.S. in Public Administration

Chief Security Officer of Brigham Young University
Instructor of Police Science, Brigham Young University
and formerly Weber State College, Ogden, Utah
Former Investigator, Los Angeles Police Department
Past President, International Association of
College and University Security Directors

CHARLES C THOMAS · PUBLISHER
Springfield · Illinois · U.S.A.

Published and Distributed Throughout the World by
CHARLES C THOMAS • PUBLISHER

BANNERSTONE HOUSE
301-327 East Lawrence Avenue, Springfield, Illinois, U.S.A.
NATCHEZ PLANTATION HOUSE
735 North Atlantic Boulevard, Fort Lauderdale, Florida, U.S.A.

With THOMAS BOOKS *careful attention is given to all details of
manufacturing and design. It is the Publisher's desire to present books
that are satisfactory as to their physical qualities and artistic possibilities
and appropriate for their particular use.* THOMAS BOOKS *will be true
to those laws of quality that assure a good name and good will.*

Printed in the United States of America
W-2

PREFACE

H AVING SERVED AS A university police chief since 1961, it has become painfully obvious to me that the amount of written information dealing with the administration of university police is rather meager. Many who are new to this specialty of law enforcement are forced to rely largely on trial and error. Some aid is obtained by discussing mutual problems at conferences, however, these are held infrequently. Having served as president of the International Association of College and University Security Directors, as well as in other positions in that organization, I have become even more cognizant of the need for written material in this field.

This book is written with the hope of making a small contribution to my profession. It is not my intent to provide a comprehensive manual of operations for university police; that can only be provided by someone conversant with the unique needs inherent to individual institutions. I have attempted to focus on general concepts which appear to be universally applicable.

For data, I have relied on my own experience as well as that of my colleagues in both the United States and Canada, and I am grateful for their aid and encouragement. Some conclusions have been based on surveys conducted in an attempt to establish concensus on certain points. My opinions have been influenced by my experience as a police officer with the City of Los Angeles where I served one year as a uniformed officer and two years as an investigator. I have also had the rich experience of serving as a permanent guest lecturer for the United States Bureau of Narcotics and Dangerous Drugs, where I have had the opportunity to discuss the role of university police with numerous deans of students who attended lecture sessions. It is largely through this experience that my views, relative to the interaction between the university police and the administration of student discipline, were formed.

It is my sincere hope that by sharing my opinions and experiences, others can possibly escape some of the difficulties that my colleagues and I have experienced.

SWEN C. NIELSEN

INTRODUCTION

T HERE IS NO lack of written material dealing with municipal police administration. An adequate selection of books treating the technical aspects of crime fighting can also be found. Most concepts from both of these fields are applicable to the university police function. This adaptation can, however, best be made with certain modifications. Such changes become desirable because of the unique atmosphere of the university. Municipalities vary from universities politically, administratively, ecologically and psychologically. For these reasons it becomes difficult to merely organize a police department at an institution of higher learning using municipal criteria, without converting certain concepts to the academic community.

Administrators faced with the task of organizing campus police units soon discover that little information, relative to adapting traditional police principles to the university community, is available. The hiring of a man to head the university police is sometimes thought to be the answer, as long as he has prior police experience.

Appointing a police chief, even one with past experience, may not be the solution. He will be facing the difficulty of adjusting his concepts to the university setting. He must resolve several issues that are not recognized in works dealing with municipal police principles.

A determination must be made relative to placing the university police within the administrative structure of the university. The issue of obtaining police authority must be met; facilities and equipment must be provided. Procedures for hiring and training personnel should be established, as well as other vital functions. These and other problems must be solved before the university police department can function adequately.

All of the above, as well as other issues, are discussed in the following pages. In order to provide valid data the opinions of numerous practitioners have been consulted. This was accomplished through several surveys and personal interviews. Most of the procedures and concepts advocated in this writing are sound and have been proven in practice by the writer and those responding to the surveys. Hopefully, the application of this knowledge will aid the reader in successfully applying traditional police management and field procedure to the university police setting.

CONTENTS

General Organizational and Administrative Concepts
for
University Police

Chapter I

SCOPE OF RESPONSIBILITY

BEFORE CONSIDERATION can be given to other administrative aspects of the university police department, its mission must be identified, since all other decisions must be made in light of that mission.

Law enforcement units on college campuses throughout the United States generally fall within two broad categories. The first is the watchman or guard type. The second is the university police department. The former is typically responsible only for the security of the physical plant and other university facilities. It has also inherited the traffic problem which has become immense on campuses during the past two or three decades. The latter type, the so-called university police, has a much broader responsibility. It functions within the university as does a municipal police department within a city. It performs all police services performed by local governments plus those functions inherent to the particular institution it was created to serve. Not only does it enforce the statutes of the state and municipality but also the university regulations regarding a variety of functions.

POLICE OR WATCHMEN?

It does not seem valid to say that one of the above-mentioned systems is better than the other. The effectiveness of the system will depend on how well the institution's needs for police services are being met. These will vary greatly depending upon the attitude of its administration. Some college administrators feel that the university student is entitled to a great deal of latitude in behavior and resist the idea of having police, university or otherwise, interfering with students' rights of experimentation.

Others are more strict and invite police action when infractions are suspected. It is understood that the attitudes reflected by college administrators are not necessarily theirs personally. They are subject to the wishes of boards of directors, trustees, etc. and receive pressure from a multitude of sources.

A realistic survey of the university's police needs should be made. If they are being adequately met with a minimal force of guards, it may not be advantageous to change. However, if it becomes apparent that needs are not satisfied, consideration should be given to broadening the activities of the existing unit, if indeed one exists. If one does not exist, consideration should be given to the creation of one.

It is apparent from information obtained that those universities with enrollment in the area of ten thousand full-time daytime students are finding their needs have not been met by the guard system. Ten thousand should not be considered a magic figure, but it reflects the size at which the municipality in which the university is located no longer satisfies the university's police needs. In some communities this figure of enrollment may be considerably lower or higher than that stated above. A survey of approximately two-hundred universities in the United States indicates this to be a reliable figure.

American universities with an enrollment of ten thousand or more full-time daytime students tend to operate police departments which provide the entire spectrum of police services. Those with fewer students tend to operate a night-watchman or guard system.

Limitations on University Police

Geographic

The university police are often limited in their sphere of operation by geographic boundaries. This limitation may be imposed by a variety of interests.

Many university administrators do not want their police officers involved in activities beyond the borders of the campus. This view is frequently shared by the police administrators of neighboring communities.

Such a rule may be unrealistic for the following reasons.

1. Criminals have never been particularly cognizant of geographical boundaries and it is unlikely that those committing crimes on the college campus are exceptions. Any ruling which limits the university police to operate only on the university property could be detrimental both to the institution and to the adjoining community.
2. The university police should be permitted to pursue law-breakers off the campus. They should be able to conduct investigations beyond the boundaries of the university, if necessary.
3. The functions of routine patrol performed by university police units should not extend off the campus unless requested by the adjoining law enforcement agency.

From a supervisory standpoint it may be difficult to restrain aggressive campus patrolmen from taking police action when they are off the campus. It should never be advocated that any law enforcement officer ignore serious violations of the law even though he is in a jurisdiction other than his own. However, minor traffic violations and the like should not be enforced by university officers while off the campus.

The problem of geographic limitation has been solved at the Brigham Young University. An agreement exists between the adjoining city, Provo, that all routine work conducted by the university police will be limited to the campus. When for any reason it becomes necessary for the campus officers to go into the city in the performance of some police function, they immediately notify the city police. It is then decided if a city officer will assist the university officer. Generally, upon notification, the city police supervisor will ask the university officer to proceed and then advise the city police of what action was taken.

To limit the university police to the campus is not realistic and can be modified to a workable agreement through mutual cooperation. The problems of university-municipal police interaction will be discussed in detail in a subsequent chapter.

Clientele

Another form of limitation is to restrict the university police to deal only with university-affiliated persons, i.e. students, faculty and staff. Many crimes are committed on university campuses by individuals who have no connection with the school at all. To limit the university police in their dealings with such persons is a questionable practice. If such a ruling were being made in reverse, that is to say, the municipal police could not handle students, its weakness becomes readily apparent.

The university police should be able to deal with any person who comes on the campus regardless of his affiliation.

RECOMMENDATIONS

The university police should be given broad responsibility for enforcing the law. Their authority should be commensurate with that responsibility. As enrollment increases the complexity of the university increases. As this occurs it is likely that the university's police needs can not be met by the traditional watchman system. The need for change should be met by the governing board requiring the administration to initiate a program so that the university will be assured of adequate police services. This can best be done by establishing a competent, university controlled police department.

The university police should not be limited in their movements or authority. Officers should be granted police authority and be permitted to make arrests wherever necessary. While routine police work should be limited to the campus, the authority granted to the university police should not.

The university police department must be staffed, equipped, organized and trained so that it can adequately perform all police services required by the campus community.

Chapter II

ORGANIZATIONAL CONCEPTS

Most concepts of municipal police organization apply to university police as well. However, one very basic organizational question must be answered for the university police: Where within the university should the police be placed administratively?

The answer generally will be that the university police chief should answer to one of the following: the Dean of Students, the Physical Plant Director, the President or a Vice President.

A survey was conducted of all the member institutions of the International Association of College and University Security Directors in 1968 to determine the national trend regarding the above question. The results of that survey are discussed later.

HISTORICAL ASPECTS

Traditionally, the campus police department was part of the physical plant department. This was primarily because the early function of the university police was limited to plant protection. The recent expanding functional scope of the university police, in many institutions, caused serious problems where the supervising administrative unit over the police remained static. As the police have been given responsibility for investigation of crimes which involve individuals from all administrative areas of the university, it becomes increasingly difficult for the physical plant director to supervise the function. He ordinarily has no responsibilities beyond the physical plant.

SURVEY FINDINGS

When the term "vice-president" is used in this writing, it is intended to describe a function rather than an ascribed title.

Grouped in this designation are a number of titular descriptions such as provost, business manager, director of personnel, etc. However, the common denominator is that they are all general officers of the institution with broad responsibilities, as opposed to the relatively narrow responsibilities of the physical plant director and the dean of students. Hereafter, the term "vice-president" will be used in the all-inclusive sense noted above.

In presenting the statistics gained from the survey, the responding universities have been grouped according to size of regularly enrolled full-time, daytime students. The groupings of the 120 responding institutions are as follows:

Group   I: Schools with enrollment of 25,000 to 37,000 (8 reporting)
Group   II: 15,000 to 22,000 (32 reporting)
Group III: 4,000 to 11,000 (58 reporting)
Group IV: 900 to 3,500 (22 reporting)

In the responding institutions 41 percent of the police departments are still under the administration of the physical plant department, and 60 percent suggest a change from there to a vice president, and in some few cases to the president. The remaining 40 percent are satisfied with their placement.

In Group I, 50 percent of the police chiefs report to the physical plant director, and 50 percent suggest a change from this status to that of reporting to a vice-president.

In Group II, 50 percent are under the supervision of the physical plant director, and of those, 55 percent advocate change to the supervision of a vice-president.

In Group III, 38 percent report to the physical plant director, and 83 percent of those advocate change to the supervision of a vice-president.

In Group IV, 33 percent of the twenty-two departments are under the supervision of the physical plant director with 28 percent advocating change.

It is interesting to note that the percentage advocating change as compared to the percentage accepting the *status quo*, as far as physical plant supervision is concerned, is almost reversed between Groups III and IV.

None of the police chiefs who are presently answering to some other office advocate that they answer to the physical plant director.

THE UNIVERSITY POLICE AS PART OF THE
DEPARTMENT OF PHYSICAL PLANT

The reasons given by university police chiefs for remaining under the physical plant director are varied. One primary reason was financial consideration. These chiefs felt it advantageous to have fiscal matters handled through the physical plant department.

Generally speaking, the physical plant department is a large department, with a concomitant large budget. Several chiefs indicate that if their budgets are prematurely depleted some money can always be found from physical plant departments to supplement them. Also, it appeared that the police budget is not so closely scrutinized by the university administration when it is contained in the overall budget of the physical plant department.

Some of the reasons given for remaining in the physical plant department, particularly by the smaller institutions, simply do not have any administrative merit. They are generally based on a feeling of mutual understanding and ability to get along with the physical plant director. Although this is an admirable situation, it can hardly be the basis for placing an organization within an institution. When the present, friendly director is not considered, the reason for being part of the physical plant department ceases to exist. Therefore it is reasonable to assume this has no administrative validity.

If only a watchman-type operation is maintained, it is administratively sound for them to be a part of the physical plant department. As one chief wrote, defending his answering to the director of physical plant, ". . . . we are charged with safety such as: campus lights, broken windows, locks, etc." If this is the scope of that particular police unit's responsibility, there is no question that their being part of the physical plant department is sound administration.

As indicated by the survey, a significant number of university police chiefs desire a transfer from the physical plant department. This is particularly true in those institutions undergoing the transition from watchmen to police oriented organizations. In their reply to the survey it is clearly sensed that the responsibilities facing their organizations, as the university expands, are beyond the limits of the physcial plant department. The police department of a large institution deals with the entire spectrum of society both from within and without the university.

The following example illustrates the aforementioned problem: Information was received by a university police department that a particular faculty member was involved in homosexual activities with a student. The student's conduct was a matter for the dean of students, and that of the faculty member was a matter for consideration by an academic dean, or possibly, the president. In neither case is it a matter to be considered by the physical plant director. The police chief needed counsel by top administrative officers in disposing of this case: would the president want an administrative hearing in the matter? Should the dean of the faculty member's college handle the matter? Should the university police investigator handle the investigation and initiate a criminal proceeding in the event that sufficient evidence was gathered? Should the dean of students question the student involved?

It is clear that the answers to the above questions, which are not particularly infrequent, would generally not lie with the physical plant director.

As this type of case develops there can be no unity of command for the police chief. He will have to consult with several people involved in the outcome of this particular type of case. Some physical plant directors would probably not want any part of such a case and would inform the security director or police chief to go elsewhere for his instructions.

Some university police chiefs are requested by top administrative officers to initiate investigations into various facets of university problems. Many deal with very delicate matters which must be kept highly confidential. The administration will sometimes violate the unity of command again, go directly to the police agency, ask for the investigation and order the police chief to report directly to them.

The investigation is then carried out and a report is made. The man who has responsibility for the organization, the physical plant director, is left totally unaware of what it is doing. It is possible that certain equipment is needed for this particular operation. The police chief cannot go to his budget officer, i.e. the physical plant director, and ask for the money, as he cannot divulge why he needs it. The administrative officer requesting the investigation may not have sufficient budget for such matters, thereby creating a frustrating situation for the police chief.

A major disadvantage voiced by some wanting a change from physical plant is that its director generally is not oriented toward police problems. His concern is building and maintenance of buildings—the planning for parking lots and roads, etc. He, in many instances, appears reluctant to make funds available for investigations into student misconduct, or crimes against persons. His preoccupation with his primary responsibility make, in effect, a stepchild of the university police unit in his department. Often the only function of the police that interested him to any noticeable degree is traffic.

Some police chiefs object to being part of the physical plant due to the lack of status afforded there. It is felt by those concerned that to place the university police officers in the same department with laborers, janitors, repairmen, etc. is an error. Interestingly enough, those citing this as a basis for being apart from the physical plant department omit listing the many highly skilled tradesmen and engineers who are also part of it. It can generally be said that students do not fully understand the way the physical plant department operates and would ascribe less status to its members than the academic staff. Since the status of an officer affects the success of his dealings with students, there may be some merit in the argument. However, it is doubtful that students are aware to whom the university police chief reports, and will probably view the police as a separate entity. It is doubtful that the status imputed to the university police officer by students will be dependent on the department to which it belongs.

Police officers in the United States have not achieved a high degree of status. There is a great hunger for this commodity within police ranks. This is the case both off as well as on the campus. Thus, advocating administrative change for the purpose of achieving status is not a surprising phenomenon. To follow such a course is folly according to Sherwood and Pfiffner, who state, "Status becomes a pathological facet of organization when it is regarded as an end in itself."[1] Administrative change based on the acquisition of status will receive no further consideration in this writing.

If a parallel were to be drawn between a university and a municipality, it would appear that the placing of the police agency under the physical plant would be unsound. It has always been held that law enforcement is an executive function. The police chief of a municipality does not answer to the director of street maintenance. Rather, he reports directly to someone in the executive branch of government, i.e. mayor, city manager or police commissioner.

In *Municipal Police Administration,* published by the International City Managers' Association, the history of American municipal police control is discussed. The evolution of control from the early practice of popular election through administrative boards, state control and commission government to unified administrative leadership is traced. In summarizing, the author states the following:

> Thus, although there is yet no absolute uniformity of practice, the trend is too clear to permit real doubt as to the ultimate result. American police administrators seem destined to be appointed by general executive officers and to exercise their proper powers free from the indecisions and confusion which go hand in hand with multiple control.[2]

It is hoped that those concerned with university police administration will learn from this dearly bought lesson without having to flounder about as did municipal police management for many years.

------

[1] Pfiffner, John M., and Sherwood, Frank P.: *Administrative Organization.* Englewood Cliffs, N. J., Prentice-Hall, Inc., 1966, p. 287.

[2] International City Managers' Association: *Municipal Police Administration.* Chicago, International City Managers' Association, 1954, p. 64.

A police agency should be separated, because of its function, from as many other groups as possible. It is to the advantage of the institution to keep the police group aloof from any intimate fraternization with other groups within the university.

The department of physical plant is sometimes the largest nonacademic department within the university. It offers great opportunity for friendships to develop between individual officers and other members of the department. This can be detrimental to the operation of truly professional police departments. It is extremely difficult for an officer to cite, arrest or otherwise cause discipline to be brought against a person with whom he bowls on the physical plant department's bowling team. This danger is, of course, not unique to those policing units which are part of the physical plant department.

It appears from the evidence gathered in the survey that there is little administrative validity in having the campus police officer as part of the department of physical plant, as long as the scope of the policing unit is one encompassing all police services rather than a watchman service.

THE UNIVERSITY POLICE AS PART OF
THE DEAN OF STUDENTS OFFICE

Some universities place the university police as part of the dean of students office. The survey indicates that no university of the eight reporting, with student enrollment between 25,000 and 37,000, has this type of organization. Of the thirty-two universities with student bodies of between 15,000 and 21,500 members, one has the police unit under the dean of students, and the police chief in this situation is advocating a change to a vice-president as his superior. Of the fifty-eight schools with student bodies of between 400 and 10,500 members, thirteen come under the direction of the dean of students. Half of the thirteen chiefs are advocating a change from the present organizational structure to being answerable to a vice-president or president. Of the twenty-two schools with student bodies of between 900 and 5,500 members, eight have the police under the dean of students. Only one of those chiefs advocates change.

Those supporting the principle of having the university police as part of the dean of students office do so on the basis of the police department's involvement with student discipline. Most questions regarding the disposition of student violators are decided by the dean of students. To have the police chief answer to him makes the task of decision making much easier. At a major Ivy League school the police chief is also an associate dean of students, but answers to the provost. The chief, in this case, states that he can make his own decisions, as he is high in the chain of command.

In small colleges where the physical plant is secured by the custodial personnel, and the police deal almost exclusively with students, there may be merit in having the university police under the dean's supervision.

In larger institutions the scope of responsibility of the university police is broader than that encountered by the dean. Therefore, it does not seem logical that he can effectively supervise it. This premise is supported by the survey in which it was found that in the responding universities with enrollments of over fifteen thousand, only one places the police in the dean of students office. It will be noted in the figures given on the preceding page that as the enrollment in the reporting institutions decreases, the number of police units under the supervision of the dean of students increases. Of all the police chiefs under his supervision 50 percent advocate change.

It is my opinion that the dean's function should be that of the adjudicator, not investigator. In the municipalities the police are not under the supervision of the judiciary. To advocate such a structure seems contrary to the American disposition. Placing the police executive in the robes of a judge would certainly meet with resistance from our civil-rights conscious society.

With the dean being oriented toward the counselling profession, some difficulty may arise between him and legally oriented university police officers. One unidentified police chief of a Southern California University with an enrollment of seventeen thousand students wrote the following on his survey response:

> We want to be able to carry out the responsibility of the department in an effective, efficient, professional manner without having to follow dictates of well-meaning but uninformed academic people.

This is how he views the supervision he receives from the dean of students who is his supervisor. He goes on and elaborates on the dean's lack of understanding regarding police matters.

In some cases, neither the dean of students nor the physical plant director is part of the highest policy-making body of the institution. Consequently they become messengers through which the police chief has contact with the general administrative officers who establish policy. The dean and director can only modify that policy within the narrow scope of their particular administrative area. The dean has some flexibility regarding student discipline, but can only receive guidance from other agencies in other matters. The physical plant director can formulate policy for the planning of streets and parking lots. He must rely on the dean of students to guide him in matters relating to student misconduct. Neither of these men has the broad powers necessary to adequately formulate the policies the police function of the university requires. If the police are expected to operate only within the confines of their respective spheres then there is no real reason for not having them as part of either entity.

THE UNIVERSITY POLICE UNDER THE ADMINISTRATION OF A VICE-PRESIDENT

Twenty-three of the fifty-eight schools with enrollment between 4,000 and 10,500 students have their police departments under the direction of a vice-president. Only one of these has the police chief answering directly to the president. In the group of universities with the smallest enrollment, 900 to 3,500, only six have the police chief answer to a vice-president. Two of those chiefs advocated that they should answer directly to the president. Only one of the chiefs in the latter group was presently answering to the president.

The most consistent reason given for answering to a vice-president was that the chief was able to obtain policy decisions quickly. A vice-president has broad authority and can make decisions encompassing the entire spectrum of university problems.

Those chiefs who advocate a change from the vice-president to the president indicate that they feel that security matters are filtered and watered down by the time they get to the president. Some feel that the security director, or police chief should sit on the highest policy-making board of the university.

The unavailability of some vice-presidents was cited as grounds for answering to someone else. Those wanting change from being under a vice-president are a minority; only four of the thirty-two police chiefs so situated advocated such a change.

A major advantage cited by those answering to a vice-president is that this places the university police chief high enough in the hierarchy that he is free from the political pressures of other campus groups.

RECOMMENDATIONS

The recommendations set forth herein are based on careful review of the information gleaned in the survey, my personal experience and discussions with my colleagues throughout the United States and Canada.

For the most effective administration of university police, the chief must be placed in a position where he answers directly to a general officer of the institution. The validity of this recommendation does not depend on the issue of student body size. Whether the school is large or small is of little consequence. The only relevant point is the scope of responsibility of the police unit. As long as it is to function as a police department, as it has been defined, it should be under the administrative supervision of either the president of the university or his executive vice-president. The choice between the two will vary from institution to institution depending largely on the span of control of the president.

An effort should be made to establish the university police as an island with an administrative bridge to a general officer.

THE PUBLIC SAFETY DEPARTMENT CONCEPT

A number of large universities have adopted the public safety department concept. They place the police, safety and fire-fighting functions in one department under one director. Each of the divisions then has a chief or captain.

This type of organization has merit in those universities where there are large staffs involved in the performance of the previously mentioned functions.

In the safety division alone there may be people involved in the task of organizing safety campaigns and educational programs for the faculty and staff. The safety personnel may also be assigned the task of investigating insurance claims against the university. The responsibility for civil defense may also fall in the safety division.

A number of universities have been forced to organize and equip a fire-fighting department. This unit may be charged with the responsibility of fighting fire as well as planning and executing a fire prevention program. In some cases they may also be assigned to conduct arson investigations.

Stanford University is an example of an institution with a fire-fighting department. It is housed in a new attractive and functional building with unusually adequate quarters for it and the university police department. Although housed together they are separated organizationally.

An example of a well-organized and operating public safety department can be seen at Michigan State University. I have had the opportunity to personally inspect this department, and was very impressed with it. If the reader has particular interest in this subject he may wish to contract the public safety director of Michigan State.

It is my conclusion that when the university becomes so large that correlation between these various safety oriented units becomes difficult, there are definite advantages in the public safety department concept.

It is not the purpose of this writing to pursue the concept of the public safety concept beyond mentioning its existence and briefly describing it. Approximately 50 percent of the university police chiefs in the United States have responsibility for campus safety as well as the law enforcement function. In interviewing several chiefs with the safety responsibility, I found that it becomes a secondary function. Most of these men are very police oriented and have little interest in developing safety programs. It is, in my opinion, unfortunate when this situation occurs. The campus safety program is too important to take a subordinate priority to the job of law enforcement. I advocate that the safety function be placed under a safety marshall who answers to the physical plant director. I do not feel that the safety and police functions should be under the same chief, except as stated above. Exactly half of the police chiefs who had the responsibility for safety wanted this task transferred to someone other than police personnel.

INTERNAL ORGANIZATION

Sir Robert Peel wrote in his famous *Guidelines for Police* that the police should be organized along military lines. Thus he wrote in 1828 just prior to the birth of the London Metropolitan Police. That concept is still largely adhered to in America.

The university police department should be no exception to this principle. The organization must be able to operate under emergency conditions without orders being questioned when issued by supervisory officers. A certain amount of military discipline is, therefore, necessary. This can best be accomplished by organizing the unit along bureaucratic lines.

Division of Tasks

The division of tasks within the university police unit will primarily be by function and time with some consideration to clientele.

The functions of the department will generally fall within three major groups: a) administrative tasks, b) line tasks, i.e. patrol, traffic and investigations and c) auxiliary tasks, i.e. communications, records and vehicle registration.

Most university police departments are of such size that the administrative tasks can be performed by the chief. A functional unit may be organized to perform each of the other major tasks. Each of these should be headed by a commander answerable to the chief. They should be given the rank of captain or lieutenant.

Under the commander of the line division it may be necessary to appoint commanders to head patrol platoons which are assigned by time. If necessary, a commander may be appointed to take charge of the detective function. I personally discourage specialization in the line division beyond that. Where large numbers of night watchmen and parking lot officers are deployed it may be necessary to appoint a supervisor for each of these functions who will answer to the line division commander.

Under the commander of the auxiliary division it may be desirable to appoint commanders to head units responsible for records and identification, communications, vehicle registration, etc. However, I reiterate that overspecialization can be detrimental to the effectiveness of any organization.

Sometimes there is a tendency to specialize within the investigative unit. While this is the practice in large municipal police departments, it cannot generally be justified in the case of small departments. The only specialization that I can personally condone, in the case of the university police, is the assigning of one officer to handle all cases dealing with drug law violations and intelligence. This function calls for unique investigative techniques and can possibly best be accomplished by having one officer responsible for it.

If the investigative function is a small one, it may be advisable to assign only one officer to this task and make him accountable to the commander in charge of the patrol division. If the investigative needs of the department proliferates, it may become necessary to establish a separate investigative division with a commander directly answerable to the chief.

After the divisional commanders have been appointed the chief must decide the order in which general responsibility for the department will fall in his absence. There does not seem to be any particular designation prescribed in this matter. The primary consideration is that the designation is made clear to all.

Military Ranks

It is advantageous to designate supervisory personnel with military ranks. Those who are so designated ought to wear the proper insignia designating their rank when in uniform. They should be addressed by their rank by all members of the department.

A number of university police departments are currently developing uniforms different from the typical police uniform. It primarily consists of a distinct blazer with some identifying emblem. The concern is to demilitarize the uniform as a public relations measure. While there is some merit to this concept it has not yet found universal acceptance.

Military rank is important to the internal efficiency of the police unit. Rank makes status designations very clear and reminds everyone of his position within the unit. It also enhances the orderly interaction with other policing agencies where military rank is invariably used. A lieutenant from a neighboring department readily recognizes his counterpart in the university police lieutenant.

The descending order of military rank for police is as follows: Chief, Captain, Lieutenant, Sergeant and Patrolman.

Some departments use a rank of corporal between sergeant and patrolman. I personally dislike this practice unless it solves some specific supervisory problem.

The rank of captain should not be used except to designate the executive police officer in the case of the public safety department. In most departments the executive officer should be designated as the chief and divisional commanders as lieutenants, skipping the rank of captain entirely. If this is not done, it is very likely that the first-line field supervisors will hold the rank of lieutenant instead of sergeant.

The uniform insignia for the various ranks may be a matter of individual taste. However, it seems that the insignia commonly used by the military would be most advantageous.

The insignia for the chief may appropriately be a general or admiral star worn on the lapel of the uniform shirt and epaulet of jackets or coats.

The sergeant rank should be used only to designate supervisory personnel—not specialists. Investigators should be designated as such or may be given the designation of "detective." This designation may be made on the officer's badge with no other distinguishing uniform insignia.

POLICE AUTHORITY

Obtaining police authority for university police departments is a perennial problem. Whenever a group of university police chiefs gather, the question will invariably be asked, "Where do you get your police authority?"

Such authority is generally derived from a state statute, or the officers are deputized by a neighboring municipal police department or sheriff's office.

A 1969 survey indicated that of eighty-six responding institutions, 85 percent had the power to make arrests. Most of them, 57 percent, derived such authority through state legislation. The others obtained it by being sworn in as special officers of the municipalities in which they were geographically located. Several universities had officers who were sworn in both by the local police department as well as the sheriff. This is typical when the university operates property which is not limited, geographically, to one jurisdiction.

If there is a choice in the matter, it is my recommendation that the university attempt to obtain police authority for its policemen through state legislation.

By being deputized by a neighboring police department, the chief, in effect, has two superiors. In this situation he is never completely free to act independently of the municipal chief whose authority he is actually exercising. This can realistically hamper the university police department's activities. The campus officer has to rely on the good will of the neighboring police chief to retain his police authority. In this way the latter may control law enforcement on the campus by threatening to revoke the commission of the university police officers.

False Arrests

Both municipal and university officials are sometimes reluctant to grant police authority to university police departments, fearing false arrest suits. The eighty-six institutions responding to the 1969 survey indicated that they collectively affected 4,781 arrests annually. Only six reported that they had ever been sued for false arrest. A judgment was rendered in only two instances, amounting to 10,000 dollars each. The other six cases had been dismissed. The reader's attention is drawn to the fact that the number of arrests reported reflects an annual number, and the false arrest cases reflect an all-time figure. The conclusion is that the likelihood of false arrest suits is remote. The problem is even more minimal when one considers the low cost of false arrest insurance protecting the university and the individual officer.

Restrictions

An attempt is sometimes made to restrict the police authority given to university officers. Generally the restriction is geographic and in some few instances limited by clientele. Either of these limitations should be discouraged.

Only 75 percent of the seventy-three university police departments with arrest power may conduct investigations off campus. Of that group approximately half may make arrests off campus.

When police authority is bestowed on university policemen it should not be restricted by geographic boundaries. Many investigations which are initiated on the campus may soon lead the officer into the municipality. It is unreasonable to require him to withdraw from the case just because it no longer is confined to the university property. The officer should be permitted to pursue the matter to its conclusion.

Limiting the university officer's authority to being exercised only against persons who are affiliated with the university is an unfortunate practice. Many crimes are committed by individuals who have no affiliation with the university, but who often perpetrate their deeds on the campus. The university officers should be able to arrest such individuals.

When a university police officer is commissioned as a peace officer, it should be on the same basis as any officer. To do less is detrimental to the university and the community.

CONCLUSION

When the law enforcement needs of the university are no longer being met by the municipal police a university police department should be established.

The university police chief should answer to someone in the administrative hierarchy with broad power, and should be responsible for providing the entire spectrum of police services.

University police officers should be commissioned to make arrests whenever and wherever crimes are committed. Their authority should not be limited by geographic or other restrictions.

The internal organization of the university police department should be along those lines generally accepted by municipal police, with adaptations to fit conditions unique to the individual institution.

Chapter III

FACILITIES AND EQUIPMENT

IT HAS BEEN MY good fortune to visit many campus police departments throughout the United States and Canada. It has become painfully obvious that most are housed in very inadequate facilities. Several universities have provided satisfactory quarters for their police department, but they seem to be in the minority. One of the most noteworthy is Stanford University; the police department and the fire department are housed in a beautiful new building. Colorado State University has provided the police department with very nice facilities in the basement of the university health center. Several others could be mentioned, but they are the exception rather than the rule.

Most quarters occupied by the university police departments are in great need of improvements. A number are housed in temporary buildings that have been vacated by others. Not only are the buildings undesirable from the standpoint of appearance, but they are too small, and cannot provide the department with the space or facilities that are required for a truly professional type of operation. Some could be renovated with a little imagination and money, others are beyond that point.

The availability of police equipment to most university police departments is also much below desirable levels. Many are operating with substandard, inefficient tools from the standpoint of efficiency as well as safety in some cases.

As the need for more sophisticated police services arises on the campus, the policing unit must be provided with the necessary tools to perform this function, as well as adequate facilities from which to operate.

HEADQUARTERS

It is a well-established principle that the police should be housed as near as possible to the center of activities requiring police attention. The university police center should be located as near the hub of campus life as possible. It should be located so that those in need of its services have easy access to its headquarters. It should be conspicuously designated with appropriate signs so that it can be easily located. Typically, however, the university police headquarters is an obscure Quonset hut in a remote location on the campus.

The facility should be manned on a twenty-four hour basis with personnel competent to assist anyone seeking service. This may be in the form of a complaint officer or a desk sergeant. In the case of smaller departments it may be in the form of specially trained dispatching personnel. These people cannot only serve the walk-in clientele, but can also answer the phones and maintain radio communications with field units.

Space Allocation

One thing that almost all police facilities have in common is lack of space. Experts in space allocation should be consulted whenever a new facility or the renovation of an old one is contemplated. Special consideration should be given to future needs so that allowances can be made for expansion.

Consideration should not only be given to floor space for office personnel, but to such things as property storage, officers' lockers and change rooms, interview and interrogation rooms, special needs of supervisory personnel, communications facilities and record storage as well.

A public counter should be provided where those seeking aid or services can be helped. Seating should be provided so that those required to wait for appointments may be accommodated. A person is often required to complete written forms, necessitating desk facilities.

Interview Rooms

A number of private interview or interrogation rooms should be made available. It is undesirable to deal with a complainant over the counter, particularly if he is upset in any way. The police personnel must have some place where they can have privacy in such cases. There they can pursue the problem without embarrassment to the complainant or the office personnel. Often matters brought to the police headquarters are of a delicate nature. No person should have to stand in a public place and be questioned.

Officers who must question suspects need the facilities required for this function. Again, this cannot be accomplished with any degree of success in an area where there are outside influences disturbing the officer's effort to ascertain truth. Interrogations are such a combination of art and science that they are performed best in a room especially constructed and equipped for that purpose. Any basic text on interrogation will give a detailed description of the special needs for an adequate interrogation room.

Communications Center

Consideration must be given to the space for a communications center. It should be constructed to exclude outside noises and to keep the radio transmissions from the general public.

It should be located in close proximity to the records of the department, as the radio dispatcher will constantly be consulting records to secure information and relay it to the units in the field. The importance of a functional communications center cannot be overstated. The radio operator is, in effect, the partner of the field officers whose only link with assistance is through the radio. It is false economy to attempt to skimp on communications equipment and facilities.

Communications centers of the most Spartan to the very elaborate designs are in use. Stanford University and the University of Northern Illinois are examples of the very finest in communications consoles. Examples of the Spartan types are too numerous to mention.

All alarm systems in use on the campus should be monitored from the university police communications center. All incoming telephone calls to the police department should be answered by the dispatcher and then referred to the party at headquarters requested by the caller. He would handle all calls for service, dispatching units in response to such requests.

Property Storage

Facilities must be provided for property storage. This applies not only to property or equipment owned by the department, but also to that property coming into police custody. The latter will generally consist either of evidence or found property.

The evidence presents a special problem. It must be stored in such a fashion that the officer seizing it can later testify in court that it could not have been contaminated or altered in any way since he took custody of it. Because most anything can be evidence, the facility for storing it should be large enough to hold such items as automobile tires, skis, furniture, etc., and yet it should contain receptacles so small that photographs, vials containing drugs, or paint chips are not lost.

The storage area must be provided with a special key to which only one or two officers have access. This is essential, as the chain of continuity regarding the evidence must be established before it is admissible at a subsequent trial.

Provision must be made for the storage of evidence between the time of seizure and the time that the person responsible for locking and managing the property closet puts it in storage. The university police at Michigan State successfully solved this problem. Lockers of the air terminal type were acquired. The key is left in the lock when the locker is empty. When an officer seizes evidence, he places it in the locker, locks it and removes the key from the lock. He then drops the key inside the locker through a slot provided for this purpose. The slot is designed so that the key cannot be retrieved without unlocking the locker. The evidence man is the only person who has the key required to open all the lockers. Upon reporting for duty each morning he unlocks the lockers and removes and processes the evidence. He stores it in the evidence closet until it is needed in court. He can then testify that he removed the property from the locked locker and has had custody of it until releasing the property for court. The seizing officer can testify that he placed the property in the locker and locked it, that he received the property prior to the trial from the evidence man and that it appears as it did when he seized it. Using this system, the chain of evidence is limited to only two men, eliminating the parade of witnesses sometimes necessary to account for the evidence.

Auxiliary Power Plant

Consideration should be given to provide the headquarters, or at least the communications center, with emergency electric power. It should be so provided that in the event of a power failure the auxiliary power plant starts automatically. It is not unusual for the power supply to be interrupted during riots or other disasters. Thus, the auxiliary plant must be installed in an area where it is secure from attack. The unit must be sufficiently powerful to generate enough power to operate the communications equipment, illuminate the facility adequately and operate a limited number of electric typewriters. Consideration should be given to future needs. The generator which will provide sufficient power for the present equipment may not be powerful enough for projected future equipment.

Restrooms

Toilet facilities should be included in the police facility. Due to their nervousness arrestees invariably need such facilities. It is undesirable to take prisoners to public facilities elsewhere. These facilities should be apart from those provided in the building for employees and the public.

The process of fingerprinting generally necessitates that a sink be placed near the area where prisoners are to be processed. University police departments not only fingerprint prisoners, but others needing fingerprints, i.e. government research clearances, ROTC, etc. In view of the obvious need to remove the fingerprint ink, it appears superfluous to indicate the need for a sink.

Miscellanous Needs

The foregoing suggestions have been of a functional nature. None of them have, in any way, advocated "gold plating."

Situations will vary from one institution to another regarding specific or unique needs. Some will have to provide for an extensive lost and found operation. Others have responsibility for the making and issuance of keys. These are important operations and will have to be incorporated into the overall plan for facilities.

Situations will vary as to how lavish the facility should be. Such decisions as to who are to have private offices, who gets carpet, the elaborateness of furniture, etc., must be made and will be limited by individual budgets.

INDIVIDUAL EQUIPMENT

Each officer will need certain basic individual equipment. Exactly what it should consist of is open to some debate. It would, however, be impossible to persuade me that the university officer needs less than what is generally considered minimal for municipal officers.

Uniform

While there is little question that the officer needs a uniform, there are varying opinions regarding of what it should consist. There are even some noteworthy exceptions to putting the officers in uniform. Yale and Princeton both refrain from this practice to some extent. The officers at these institutions are dressed in civilian suits.. At Yale they wear dress hats along with the suit. With the mode of dress seen on many campuses, this is almost as distingiushing as the traditional police uniform.

It is generally agreed that the uniform worn by the university police should be distinctly different from the neighboring police departments. Again, this opinion is not a unanimous one. Michigan State university police wear a uniform similar to neighboring departments. However, this is a unique exception.

The usual argument for different uniforms is that the departments, both university and municipal, want to retain their autonomy, and sometimes guard it rather jealously.

Policy for Supplying Uniforms

There are two major programs for supplying uniforms to the officer. One is that of simply issuing the uniforms and equipment to the new officer and replacing them upon evidence of fair wear and tear. The other alternative is to provide a uniform allowance paid monthly to the individual officer and then requiring him to purchase his own uniforms and equipment to conform to standards set by the department.

The advantage of the issuance program is that the officer tends to look better, as he will freely ask to have uniforms or equipment replaced when worn or damaged. When an officer is given an allowance for uniforms it, in effect, becomes part of his salary. He may use it for groceries rather than for uniforms. Supervisory personnel may be hesitant to demand that uniforms be replaced as they recognize that the money is really coming from the family budget.

Officers who are assigned to work in plain clothes may be discriminated against under the issuance system. This occurs when they are required to furnish their own work clothes while those assigned to uniform divisions are furnished theirs at no cost. Where the allowance system is used this problem is eliminated somewhat. Where the uniformed officers are required to purchase uniforms that can only be used while on duty; the plain clothes officer can purchase clothes that can be used while off duty as well as on.

Having had experience with both systems, I advocate the issuance program. Some compensation can be made in the salaries of officers who are assigned to work "plain clothes" to compensate for the inequity this may present. Under the issuance program the officers look sharper and proper supervision is enhanced by eliminating the problem mentioned above, relative to replacing worn or damaged parts.

Uniform needs will vary a great deal depending on climate and individual tastes. Smartness, comfort and durability are prime considerations when choosing uniforms. Consideration must also be given to the functional aspects of the uniform. It would be detrimental to design a uniform coat, for example, which makes it difficult for the officer to reach his weapon.

Basically, the officer will need at least two changes of uniforms. Consideration must be given to issuing a winter uniform, as well as one to be worn during hot weather. Each man should also be provided with special clothing to be worn during inclement weather.

Headgear

In recent years a trend has developed among municipal police departments toward the use of helmets for general duty. This type of headgear has replaced the more traditional police uniform cap in several areas. It is my opinion that university police officers should have these issued, but that they should be worn only during special events drawing large crowds, especially if the crowd is likely to be particularly volatile. A relatively inexpensive face shield can be purchased which easily attaches to the general duty helmet, making it very practical for use when facing disorderly crowds.

Helmets have been worn by officers of the Brigham Young University Police with no adverse responses. They have been in use approximately five years, being donned only as outlined above.

Uniform Insignia

As indicated earlier, the rank insignia used on the university police uniforms should be compatible with that used by the neighboring police departments. It may be desirable to design a shoulder patch with a design compatible with other symbols of the institutions. Some departments have colorful attractive shoulder insignia, which is generally a matter of individual taste.

Individual Weapons

When considering individual equipment for the university police officer, the question of weapons will arise. Should the campus officer be armed? If so, with what?

It is doubtful that the question of arming university policemen can be decided without emotional objection from the academic world. However, it is inconceivable to most law enforcement officials to ask any officer to apprehend violators of the law without being armed. While professors may distinguish between municipal officers who are armed and university police officers who are unarmed, it is very doubtful that a criminal will.

The most tragic result of not arming university police occurred on the University of Texas Campus at Austin during August, 1966. After being confronted by an unarmed university police officer, a gunman killed twelve and wounded thirty-one people while using a rifle from a tower on the campus. He was finally killed by an armed policeman from the City of Austin. It is possible that had the university officer been armed these lives could have been saved, and the injuries prevented.[3]

Mr. John C. Marchant, Director of Security at the University of Massachusetts, conducted a survey in December of 1968 regarding the use of firearms, aerosols and gasses by university police departments. He received responses from 140 institutions and concluded the following:

> With respect to the carrying of sidearms by campus police, little difference was reflected between those institutions having a majority of resident students and those reporting a majority of commuting students. At the urban institutions 75 percent carried sidearms at all times and 16 percent did not carry sidearms at any time. On suburban campuses 67 percent of the institutions reported that campus police carried sidearms at all times, while only 10 percent reported that campus police did not carry sidearms at any time.
>
> Responses relating to enrollment indicated that the percentage of campus police who carried sidearms at all times noticeably increased when the student body exceeded 5,000.

Marchant further indicates that relative to shotguns and rifles, nine departments carry them in their patrol vehicles, thirty-eight institutions have them available for emergency use, while ninety-eight have none available.

Regarding Mace and tear gas he reports that of the 140 schools responding, forty-nine have their officers carry this type of weapon on his person, sixteen carry them in their patrol vehicles, fifty-four have them available for emergency use, while fifty-six have none available.

Consideration should be given to equipping the university officer with the police baton. This proposal will also provoke

---

[3] Nevin, David: Charlie Whitman: The Eagle Scout Who Grew Up With A Tortured Mind. *Life*, August, 1966, pp. 28-29.

controversy on the campus as it has elsewhere. It is the contention of many officers that the baton is the most effective police weapon, and yet it is considered a symbol of brutality by many. An expert, Mr. Robert Koga, has written the following:

> The baton is the most controversial weapon in the police arsenal. Neither the revolver nor the shotgun stirs the emotional criticism generated by the use of the baton.
>
> Its critics call it a nightstick, a riotstick, a baton or a billyclub. Whatever label they attach to it, their complaint is over its use as a club.
>
> The word "club" has a primitive connotation. The club is one of the oldest weapons devised by man; predated, perhaps, only by the throwing of rocks. The strength and the success of protest against law enforcement's use of the baton lies principally in its comparison to the primitive club.
>
> Used properly, the baton is one of the most effective and *humane* weapons in the police arsenal. Improper use is certain to lead to its eventual abolishment.[4]

If the baton is to be used by any policing agency, adequate training is essential. The Brigham Young University Police have used batons since 1961 without any incident or improper use being alleged against any officer. The weapon has been a deterrent on many occasions where an attack against an officer had been contemplated.

The training given the officers at Brigham Young is that outlined by Mr. Koga, quoted above. This method not only teaches the officer the pragmatic aspects of how to handle the baton, but also conditions him in the art of self-control, which is essential when an officer is placed in a situation where he must use force against any person.

It is my firm opinion that there is no adequate basis for not arming university police officers merely because they are charged with the responsibility of policing a college campus. If the arming of the officers is being objected to on the basis of incompetence then there may be cause. However, this should not be a reason for not arming the men, but the reason for improving them.

------

[4] Koga, Robert K., and Nelson, John G.: *The Koga Method: Police Baton Technique.* Beverly Hills, Calif., The Glenco Press, 1968, p. 1.

It is also my firm opinion that the introduction of any piece of equipment, including weapons, must be preceded by adequate training. In the case of weaponry it is not enough to teach the officers how to use them. When to use them must also be given adequate attention.

Each officer's job should depend on his demonstrated ability to handle all equipment safely and effectively.

AUTOMOTIVE EQUIPMENT

Deciding what type and make of motor vehicle to use for campus patrol can be difficult, as it is in a municipality. On one hand are those advocating the very exotic police interceptors with very powerful engines and elaborate optional equipment. On the other hand we find those who insist that this function can be accomplished by the use of three-wheeled scooters or other "economical" conveyances.

To arrive at a realistic conclusion, the mission of the university patrol force should be examined carefully. It is foolish to compare one campus against another. Some have miles of road to patrol while others have none.

If the vehicle is for no other purpose than transporting an officer from one building to another for his nightwatchman's rounds, it would be unwise to equip him with a sophisticated patrol cruiser. It is equally unwise to expect a patrolman charged with the responsibility of traffic enforcement on an extensive road net to use a three-wheeled motor scooter.

The vehicle most generally used for routine patrol in the United States is the four-door sedan. The argument in favor of the four-door unit is that it facilitates the transporting of prisoners, victims and witnesses. If the probability of transporting anyone is slight, it may be wise to consider a two-door sedan, particularly if a better price can be obtained than in the case of the four-door sedan.

The issue of horsepower will be raised when patrol vehicles are discussed. While it is difficult to establish the exact amount needed, it can be said that it ought to be an eight cylinder engine rather than a six. This is particularly important if the unit is to be used for any type of high-speed response.

In 1958 the Los Angeles Police Department conducted a survey of 408 high-speed pursuits. The results of the survey are as follows:

> Eighty-three percent or 338 of 408 were successful.
>
> Seventy-one percent or 241 of 338 of the successful pursuits were made by police vehicles equipped with V-8 engines.
>
> Twenty-nine percent or 97 of 338 of the successful pursuits were made by police vehicles equipped with 6-cylinder engines.
>
> Ninety percent or 63 of 70 of the unsuccessful pursuits were made by police vehicles equipped with 6-cylinder engines.
>
> Ten percent or 7 of 70 of the unsuccessful pursuits were made by police vehicles equipped with V-8 engines.
>
> Even more significant is the breakdown of the successful pursuits by the reason given for the success. Twelve of the successful 6-cylinder pursuits ended by reason of a traffic accident to the pursued vehicle, as opposed to one such occurrence in a V-8 pursuit . . .
>
> Regardless of engine type, one important factor in pursuit driving is suspension and braking. Police vehicles with heavy duty suspension and brakes can often gain valuable distance on a more powerful car at corners.[5]

While operating a police vehicle under emergency conditions, the officer needs to be able to concentrate on the road ahead, as well as using his radio. His safety and that of all others on the road is enhanced, if the vehicle is equipped with an automatic transmission. It can safely be said that the automatic transmissions now on the market are so engineered that their maintenance is probably more economical than that required for standard transmissions. The automatic transmission is especially suited for the type of driving involved in routine patrol, i.e. stop-go and slow driving.

The vehicle must be equipped with every safety device available. Such items as seat belts and head rests should be standard equipment in any patrol vehicle. Considerations may even be given to roll bars, as the current trend in automotive engineering seems to be toward a structurally weak top.

---

[5] Gourley, G. Douglas, and Britow, Allen P.: *Patrol Administration*. Springfield, Ill., Charles C Thomas, 1966, pp. 204-5.

As a former Los Angeles Police Officer with several pursuits to my credit, accounting for some of the statistics quoted in the study on the previous page, I strongly urge serious consideration be given to the purchase of police vehicles that are specifically built as such. Several manufacturers have a "police package" available. The special equipment that these units are provided with enhances their road worthiness by providing improved suspension, brakes, steering, etc. They are sold with a variety of engine sizes.

The Brigham Young University Police have purchased such vehicles for several years and have experienced great satisfaction both from a tactical and maintenance standpoint.

Police Vehicle Accessories

Aside from the usual optional equipment, the patrol unit will require some special equipment. The most basic is the two-way radio. There are a variety of radios on the market. The prospective buyer is wise to choose from well-established American products. More consideration will be given to the question of communications equipment in a later chapter.

Shotgun

A twelve-gauge shotgun should be mounted within easy reach of the driver. There are several electric, as well as keyed, locking devices on the market. These will hold the weapon securely in the vehicle in such a fashion that the officer can easily remove it when needed.

The shotgun can easily be mounted in the driver's vicinity without it being readily visible from outside the vehicle.

First Aid Supplies

Adequate first aid supplies must be placed in the patrol vehicle. The guidance of the university health center should be obtained to determine what type of supplies should be carried. They should be placed in a kit which can easily be removed from the vehicle whenever the officer is responding to an injury case.

Fire Extinguishers

Fire extinguishers should be installed in all police cars. The police officer will often be the first unit responding to a fire alarm. He can often minimize fire loss and injury if he is equipped and trained to deal with a fire while yet in its early stages. With the exotic fuels used currently, automobile fires are not uncommon, and the officer must be equipped to deal with this problem.

Emergency Lights and Siren

The vehicle must be equipped with emergency lights and audible signals as required by law. Each state has its own specifications of what constitutes an emergency vehicle. The college police administrator will have to determine what these requirements are and then comply.

To eliminate drilling holes in the roofs of police cars, bars are available on which all emergency equipment can be fastened. The bars then fasten to the raingutters of the vehicle, and can easily be transferred to replacement vehicles, eliminating some of the depreciation of the discarded ones brought about by the holes commonly caused by permanently attaching emergency equipment.

Marked Versus Unmarked Patrol Vehicles

There are differing opinions on the advisability of marked, as opposed to unmarked patrol cars. My stand is that the conspicuously marked patrol vehicle is advantageous.

The marked vehicle aids in the attempt to create a feeling of omnipresence of police. One of the basic functions of police patrol is the repression of crime. This can most effectively be accomplished through conspicuous patrol. It seems rather elementary that this can be done best by vehicles that are readily recognized as patrol vehicles.

In switching from unmarked to marked vehicles at Brigham Young University, the police there received several comments and questions about "all those new police cars." There were those who were critical of the university for being so heavily policed. Only one car had been purchased and marked, but it could no longer pass unnoticed.

By clearly marking police cars, citizens can easily recognize them when needing assistance. This is especially significant when dealing with visitors to the campus in need of directions or other information.

The marked vehicle also has an advantage from a supervisory standpoint. The patrol officer cannot hide with a marked vehicle. He is kept in the public eye which may cause him to be more attentive to duty. He is less likely to violate the rules of the road, as he knows that people in the academic world are not timid about reporting misconduct of officers.

Some officers will argue that they cannot write any citations when patrolling in a marked vehicle. This may be true. It should, however, be kept in mind that his function is not to write citations, but to reduce accidents and crime. Citations are only one means for reducing accidents; conspicuous patrol is another. The latter function will act as a constant reminder to motorists that the road is patrolled. This, hopefully, will make him more cognizant of his driving. It reduces accidents without the negative aspects of citing a motorist. Most motorists will admit that whenever they see a patrol car they promptly check the speedometer. It is, of course, not expected that the use of marked cars will totally eliminate the need for issuing citations.

The police cannot be accused of the "unsportsmanlike conduct" of sneaking up on unsuspected motorists if they are using well-marked patrol vehicles. This concern with fair play is a real factor in the overall public relations program of the department.

It cannot be denied that certain crime problems may arise where the use of unmarked patrol vehicles is not an advantage. However, for routine patrol the marked patrol car is advocated.

If university police departments mark their vehicles it should be done in such a fashion as to distinguish them from the units of neighboring police departments.

Use of Nonpatrol Vehicles

Vehicles used only for transportation need not be as elaborately equipped as the patrol units. They should be equipped with a two-way radio, siren and red light, as minimal equipment. The vehicle best suited for this type of function is a standard four-door sedan with a V-8 engine and an automatic transmission. If the unit will not be used for tailing or surveillance, a six-cylinder engine may be sufficient.

These vehicles would be used mostly by follow-up investigators in their contacting parties to an incident under investigation. The unmarked car is particularly advantageous when officers are contacting people at their residences. The presence of a marked police vehicle in front of a person's home is often the subject of neighborhood talk, and will not make any friends for the department.

If the vehicle is to be used for surveillance and tailing, it should be equipped with switches whereby one headlight and tail lights can be turned off while the vehicle is in use. This has the effect of altering the appearance of the vehicle at night. Vehicles used for this purpose should be as nondescript as possible. Sometimes officers want a very odd looking car so as to avoid the stereotype plain police car. These "cool cars" often become known and are easily distinguished from other vehicles on the road. In such cases the coolness of the car will work to the detriment of the officer.

Motorcycles

The three-wheeled motorcycle has a definite place in the campus police automotive fleet. It is an excellent unit for checking parking lots. It can be equipped with a radio with little difficulty, thereby enhancing its value in the field. It can be bought with a body capable of carrying flares, barricades and accident investigation gear. It can be bought with a rider enclosure, giving the operator protection from inclement weather. A variety of heaters can be installed in the driver's compartment, making it an all-weather unit.

It is my opinion that there is little justification for the use of two-wheeled motorcycles by university police. Stanford University is the only institution known to me where they are used. Considering the hazard to the officer riding it, the cost of the unit is exorbitant. The operating cost is even higher in areas where the weather precludes the use of the unit during inclement periods.

Aside from hazards to the officer, Gourley and Bristow list the following disadvantages of solo motorcycle patrol:

1. Cannot be used in inclement weather.
2. Cannot be fully utilized over a twenty-four hour period as individual motorcycles are usually assigned to individual officers.
3. No longer can pursue automobiles with past success.
4. Cannot carry sufficient police equipment.
5. Does not lend itself to the best mobile communications.
6. Cannot transport prisoners.[6]

Unless the motorcycle is assigned to the patrolling of extremely congested areas in climates where the weather permits almost limitless use, the motorcycle is not recommended.

COMMUNICATIONS EQUIPMENT

Officers are often heard commenting, "How did they ever do police work without radios?" The wonder of the automobile must take second place to radio communications as being a boon to law enforcement. Modern law enforcement would grind to a complete halt within minutes of communications failure.

With the advent of the one-man patrol unit, the need for adequate radio communications is even more acute than in the days of two-man or squad cars. The radio dispatcher becomes, in effect, the partner of the officer in the one-man patrol unit. This not only emphasizes the importance of adequate radio equipment, but the dispatcher's competence as well.

I know of no university police department which routinely uses two-man patrol units. Consequently, all recommendations made relative to communications will be with the one-man patrol unit in mind.

Communications equipment will be discussed in very broad terms. The technical aspects of police communications equipment is much too complicated for a general consideration of

---

[6] Gourley and Bristow, p. 214.

police administration. Those seeking specific technical assistance should contact a reputable electronics firm or a police communications equipment dealer.

Base Station

A base station should be installed at the university police headquarters. Preferably, it should be manned around the clock with someone who has no other responsibility than that of answering the phones and handling radio communications. The station must be of sufficient power to adequately cover the area policed. Before any equipment is purchased, the department should carefully consult the Federal Communications Commission regulations relative to power, antenna height and other limitations. The equipment should be such as to facilitate quick, reliable information dissemination to field units.

Keeping these primary considerations in mind, the department should carefully review all equipment available on the market. It is relatively easy to overbuy in radio equipment. There are numerous gadgets available that do not materially enhance the capabilities of the equipment.

Mobile Radios

Each vehicle used by the university police should be equipped with three-way radios. This makes it possible for the units to talk to each other as well as to the base station. This is an essential feature as it makes it possible to correlate the efforts of responding field units to the same incident. Again, it is not feasible to state the exact type or make of equipment that ought to be installed. This will vary on the range requirements and other technical considerations.

Portable Radios

In addition to the base station and mobile radios, it is highly desirable to have some portable radios available. They should be on the same radio frequency as the other radios. The portable radios should be of such power that they can be heard by all other radios in use. Nickel cadmium batteries are desirable as they permit the radios to be recharged, eliminating the need for stocking conventional batteries. Multiple unit chargers are available into which the whole radio is placed while out of service.

A variety of components are available for these radios. By carefully planning the purchase of these the portable radio can be a very versatile unit. Individual dealers should be contacted for demonstrations when the purchase of portable radios is contemplated.

Radio Maintenance

Some radio dealers have contract maintenance available also. It has, in my experience, not been practical to have the electronic repair shop on the campus maintain police radios. These radios are very sophisticated and require a great amount of special equipment and factory trained experts. Federal regulations relative to frequency variations are such that the radios need regular checking for frequency deviation. Failure to do so places the department's radio license in jeopardy.

Contract maintenance can be designed to meet the specific needs of the department. The cost of such a contract will probably seem exorbitant to the novice, but it is money well spent on an essential facet of the police operation.

Radio Frequency Availability

Obtaining an adequate radio frequency may be a serious problem. This is especially true in the case of private institutions. They do not generally qualify under the regulations of the FCC for frequencies available to public safety organizations. Some departments are overcoming this problem by using a frequency which is assigned to a neighboring department. Another alternative is to use those frequencies available to private businesses, or citizen band frequencies. These possibilities do not present a good solution. Neither provides privacy, as these frequencies are available to almost anyone. At almost any toy store a child can buy a radio which is tuned to one of these frequencies. The power authorized is totally inadequate for most police functions. The university police departments forced to use a business frequency can look forward to sharing it with delivery trucks, cement trucks, pizza parlors and others. The inadequacy of this arrangement is obvious.

Representing a private university, I have had the experience of obtaining a public safety radio frequency. It was obtained only after a two-year legal effort wherein the FCC was persuaded that such a frequency was needed. This need was established by showing that the function of the university police, although operated by a private institution, was in fact a public safety function and therefore should be granted the advantage of a suitable radio frequency.

SPECIALIZED POLICE EQUIPMENT

The list of desirable equipment for the university police department is almost endless. An attempt will be made in this section to describe some of the tools needed to operate a competent police organization.

Riot Equipment

With the possibility of a violent confrontation being a likelihood, the university police must be equipped to deal with such an incident.

Helmets

Each officer should be issued a helmet. There are a variety of adequate helmets on the market. Some have face and ear shields and other features protecting the wearer.

While these helmets are excellent for riots, they can be used for little else. Consideration should be given to the purchase of general duty helmets. They can be worn on a variety of occasions where the regular riot helmet would be inappropriate. A number of police departments have adopted general duty helmets as their regular head wear. In 1963 Lt. Alena of the Pasadena Police Department stated during a personal interview that his department had experienced a 12 percent decrease in man-days lost to on-duty injuries per year, since wearing helmets at all times. The injuries that had most dramatically been reduced were those sustained in traffic accidents and assaults on officers.

There may be some objection to university police officers wearing helmets routinely. However, there is adequate reason for wearing helmets on special occasions. If such occasions are chosen with care, in my opinion they would be minimal.

The F. Morton Pitt Co., of San Gabriel, California has developed a face shield which attaches to the general duty helmet very quickly. This makes the helmet a very adequate piece of riot equipment.

Gas Masks

All personnel should be issued gas masks. It is essential to have this piece of equipment for riot control, as well as for other situations. There are a number of adequate gas masks on the market. Consideration should be given to comfort, simplicity and adequate visibility.

A problem of communicating arises when wearing a gas mask. Speech is badly muffled by it, particularly when trying to use a radio. The only way to overcome this problem is to install a microphone inside the mask. A cord will have to be installed through the face of the mask. A portable radio can then be utilized without muffling the broadcast.

It may not be practical to install microphones in all the gas masks, but those assigned to supervisory personnel should be given priority.

Chemical Weapons

Tear gas and other chemical weapons should be part of the university police arsenal. While there may be some controversy over the use of Mace and its effectiveness, there is little doubt regarding the effectiveness of conventional tear gas. An adequate supply of gas should definitely be kept on hand. More than one delivery system should be available, consisting of hand grenade canisters as well as projectile types. Projectiles can be fired by special gas guns as well as grenade launchers which attach to conventional firearms.

When stocking gas it should be kept in mind that when gas is to be used in the field, sufficient amounts must be employed. Less than an adequate barrage of gas is almost worse than none.

Miscellaneous Riot Equipment

Plans, facilities, transportation and equipment for handling mass arrests are a must. A disposable, one-use, hand restraining device can be bought at low cost. It is sold under the name Flexi-Cuff®, and has been used with great success by a number of university police departments. At Michigan State several arrestees attempted to burn the plastic Flexi-Cuffs using cigarettes, resulting only in burns to the individuals.

Still and motion picture cameras must be available as part of the riot equipment. If these cannot be purchased by the police department, arrangements should be made with some other agency to furnish equipment and operators, if necessary.

When mass arrests are anticipated the dialogue between officers and arrestees should be recorded on tape. The demeanor of an unruly group can be demonstrated in court by taping the sounds from the group.

Anti-Sniper Equipment

The organization, training and equipping of an anti-sniper squad should be considered carefully. It is suggested that it consist of four officers with two alternates. Each man should be equipped with a steel helmet, painted dull black, body armor and dark jump suits.

One man is the "spotter." He is equipped with his personal sidearm and a portable radio. He also carries a pair of good binoculars.

His function, as his title connotes, is that of spotting the sniper and directing the movements of the squad.

The second man is the protector. Besides his personal sidearm, he is armed with a short barreled shot gun with pump action. His duty is to protect the squad from dissidents on the ground.

The third officer is armed with an automatic or semi-automatic weapon. His function is to give the squad cover fire while moving. He is not expected to knock the sniper down, but merely to pin him down during the time of exposure.

The fourth member of the group is the rifle man. He is

armed with a high power rifle with a variable power scope. His function is to hit the sniper.

This squad, with its alternates, must train constantly. Not only must its members be thoroughly familiar with their equipment, but with each other as well. Each member must be able to use the equipment assigned to the other members of the squad.

Traffic Radar

On campuses where speeding automobiles become a problem, the traffic radar can be of great help. I have had the experience of introducing radar on a college campus and found absolutely no resistance to it. It appears that the use of radar in enforcing speed laws has been accepted by almost everyone. Prior to introducing it on the campus, a nationwide survey was conducted, showing that radar was used by several universities without difficulty.

Alarm Systems

As the size and diversity of the physical plant increases, the question of alarm systems may arise. While alarms cannot replace personnel, they can enhance plant protection systems where only night watchmen are used.

Alarms can be designed to monitor almost anything. They can detect intruders, temperature variances, flooding, water flow, electric current variances and radioactivity levels.

The entire system should terminate at and be monitored by the police dispatcher. This facilitates the promptness of proper response to the alarm.

It is impossible to say what model of alarm is best. There are a variety of systems available, ranging from the very simple to the very sophisticated.

The prospective customer can find ample advertising in any periodical dealing with industrial security matters. It is advisable to have several manufacturers demonstrate their equipment before deciding on any one of them.

Particular attention should be given to the sensitivity of the sensory devices which activate the alarm. They must be sensitive enough to function when necessary. However, oversensitive equipment can become extremely bothersome. It will result in false alarms, lessening officers' vigilance. Becoming conditioned to false alarms can be extremely dangerous. There is also the practical aspect of wasted time spent in investigating false alarms.

The installation of alarm systems should be approached from a campus standpoint rather than by individual buildings. Unless a campus-wide plan is followed, it is possible that a piecemeal approach will produce a number of sub-systems, none of which can be integrated into a comprehensive campus system capable of being monitored at one central terminal.

Photographic Equipment

Photography is an essential component of modern law enforcement. It is predicated on the purchase or availability of adequate equipment and its use.

It is difficult to say what equipment is best, with individual photographers vehemently defending their own choices. The opinion of Mr. Leland V. Jones, recently retired Assistant Professor of Police Science at the State College of California at Los Angeles, does seem to carry some weight, however. After twenty-eight years' experience in the crime laboratory of the Los Angeles Police Department where he gleaned personal experience in some ten thousand cases and about 2,500 personal appearances as a witness in court, he states the following:

> Photographic equipment used for field work by a police laboratory should be the best obtainable. This does not necessarily mean the most expensive. A good lens costs money, but it is one of the best investments that can be made and is one part of the camera that should never wear out. Shutters must be accurate and dependable, as shutter failure can be disastrous. The camera itself should be of rigid construction and should afford an ease of operation. Probably the best field camera is a press or graphic type. It is easy to operate, is of rigid construction, and has become very popular in all field photography. A camera should be synchronized for flash, but photofloods are also a necessary component of a complete field kit. There are many types of photography at crime scenes where the latter is absolutely essential. The kit should also include a very sturdy tripod of such a type as to enable the camera to be pointed perpendicular to the floor for photographing footprints, etc. A short tripod capable

of lowering the camera so that photographs may be made in a horizontal plane of objects such as hub caps, bumpers, etc., is a valuable addition to a field kit. The kit should also include a fifty foot tape and six inch rulers, the latter in various colors, including one of transparent plastic. It should also include film holders containing various type film.

If the assets of the department will permit, a 35 mm camera, loaded with color, will be found excellent for accurately reproducing the scene. Some of the better cameras of this type are the Contax® and Leica®, yet excellent results may be obtained with a less expensive camera such as an Argus® or an Eastman®. Twenty color photographs of this type cost only about three dollars and are very effective if projected in court.[7]

Another camera that should be mentioned is the Polaroid Land Camera®. While it is not suited for general crime scene coverage, it has some features that make it a valuable law enforcement tool.

Its relative simplicity makes it a camera that can be used by the patrol officer in the field. The instant picture assures him that he has a good picture, and if not, he can take another. The primary value of the polaroid picture is in cases where it is desirable to have a picture; yet a subsequent court presentation is unlikely. Damage in minor accidents, or safety hazards may fall within this category.

Equipment for taking motion pictures should also be available to the university police. To purchase such equipment may be unwise. In order to take adequate motion pictures, good equipment is a must. This type of photography also requires expertise generally not possessed by someone other than a professional photographer. Possibly arrangements can be made with some other agency on the campus willing to make the equipment and personnel available to the police when such pictures are needed.

Criminalistics Equipment

Generally speaking, it would be impractical for the university police to establish a complete criminalistics laboratory. Beyond

---

[7] Jones, Leland V.: *Scientific Investigation and Physical Evidence.* Springfield, Ill., Charles C Thomas, 1959, pp. 87-88.

some basic, field testing equipment the criminalistic needs can be met either by state or federal crime laboratories. In some cases the university chemistry or physics departments can be of great value in analyzing evidence. I am personally indebted to several professors who have analyzed evidence and later testified in court.

It has become essential to have field tests for identifying narcotics and dangerous drugs. These tests are not absolute, but merely guide the officer. For final analysis the university's own chemistry laboratory can be of assistance. The chemist will need some samples of known drugs to use for standards. These can be obtained through some state agencies or through the United States Justice Department, Bureau of Narcotics and Dangerous Drugs (BNDD). For assistance the university police chief should contact the nearest BNDD Field Office.

Other criminalistics kits that may be of value are those used for detecting blood, semen and obliterated serial numbers on metals. It is also desirable to have some equipment for doing preliminary examinations of questioned documents.

Dactylography

All university police units should have the equipment necessary to develop and lift latent fingerprints. The value of fingerprints to criminal investigation is so well established that any further mention of it seems superfluous. However, it is essential to have adequate equipment. It should contain a number of multi-colored powders for greater background contrast to aid in photographing latent prints. Implements for developing latent prints on paper should also be provided.

Polygraphy

While the use of a polygraph is a controversial matter, it cannot be denied that when used properly by a competent ethical examiner it is a valuable investigative tool. The cost of purchasing the instrument and adequately training an examiner may be prohibitive to the average university police department. Possibly, the services of a competent examiner can be retained, when necessary, from some other agency.

As a graduate of the Gormac Polygraph Course at Pasadena, California, I have used a polygraph on many cases. It is gratifying to report that in almost all cases the subjects were cleared when tested by the polygraph method.

The instrument should be used only when all other investigative routes have been exhausted. In all cases it must be used only with the full consent of the suspect, with no implicit or explicit coercion of any kind. The suspect's refusal to submit to an examination must never be construed, officially or otherwise, as an implied admission. It is interesting to note that almost all the examinations I have administered have been upon the request of the suspect, and not at the urging of the investigator or other university personnel.

The polygraph has been very valuable in cases, such as dorm thefts, where there are a number of suspects who each had the opportunity for committing the crime. If they severally will agree to take a polygraph examination, the number of suspects can be reduced dramatically.

The successful use of the polygraph will often hinge on the ability of the investigators. Developing a case in such a manner that it can be adapted to polygraph application, takes special skill. A tendency may develop, on the part of the investigators, to rely on the polygraphist instead of on conventional investigative procedure. This is particularly true in the case of a weak investigator who may use the polygraph as a threat against a suspect for the purpose of obtaining an admission or confession.

It is the police chief's responsibility to see that the officers of the department are adequately trained in the applicability of the polygraph, not only from a technical standpoint, but from an ethical one as well.

Surveillance Equipment

During the 1967 term, in the case of *Katz v. United States,*[8] the United States Supreme Court decided that the question of electronic surveillance was not one of trespassing, as it had formerly held in *Silverman v. United States,*[9] but rather one of

---

[8] Katz v. United States, 389 U.S. 347 (1967).

[9] Silverman v. United States, 365 U. S. 505 (1961).

search and seizure, thereby bringing it under the purview of the Fourteenth Amendment.

Commenting on Katz, Professor Nedrud states the following:

> Katz gave meaning to the Berger decision of the 1966 Term. It held that privacy may be invaded even in a public telephone booth by a listening device attached to the outside thereof. But its clarification that eavesdropping in fact would be countenanced by the Court with the means by which compliance could be effected was far the more important part of the decision since until Katz the likelihood of eavesdropping under Berger was nil.[10]

The Berger case referred to above, is a case dealing with a wiretapping case in New York State, where this practice was ruled unconstitutional.[11]

The practical aspect of the Katz Case is that under certain circumstances an officer can obtain a warrant permitting him to employ electronic surveillance. This is done under the same authority and restrictions as are imposed when executing a regular search and seizure warrant. It must be recognized that the issuance of such a warrant is dependent on a specific state statute enabling such issuance.

If the officer can successfully obtain such a warrant, he will, of course, need the equipment to detect and record the conversation. This may require some rather exotic equipment and a considerable amount of training in its operation. Both must be provided if the institution concerned decides that it will venture into this area of investigation.

The appropriateness of this type of investigation on a college campus is one that can probably never be settled. However, when conditions on college campuses result in murder and mass destruction of property, it might be said that such extreme behavior warrants vigorous investigation employing every means sanctioned by the courts.

It is not the purpose of this writing to resolve the ethical question of electronic eavesdropping, but to merely point out that it may be legal, and in some cases justifiable. Without the

---

[10] Nedrud, Duane R.: *The Criminal Law 1968. Chicago*, L. E. Publishers, Inc., 1968, p. Com-38.

[11] Berger v. New York, 87 Sup. Ct. 1837 (1967).

proper devices for carrying out such activity, the question is rather moot. There are a variety of gadgets on the market which will permit eavesdropping on almost all conversations. If the university police decides that such equipment is desirable, one reputable supplier is the Fargo Company in San Francisco, California.

One piece of equipment falling in this category is a tape recorder. While it may not necessarily be used for any covert purpose, no policing agency should be without one. There are a variety of very adequate instruments on the market. While there are a number of optional features available on most recorders, many of them are superfluous and would have no value to the law enforcement task. It should be lightweight, sturdy and operable with or without batteries.

Departmental Library

Each law enforcement agency should have an adequate library. A good library will not only help the chief in his planning and decision making, but is a must for the preparation of training materials.

While it is difficult to specifically name those books that are essential, some general conclusions can be drawn. The library should contain books containing state and local criminal statutes. The department should also subscribe to a monthly service providing current case decisions by both state and federal appellate courts.

It must be remembered that all statute books must be updated each time the legislature meets. This can generally be done by purchasing a supplement to the parent volume, rather than replacing the entire volume.

Several basic police science texts should be provided. These deal with such subjects as patrol procedure, investigative techniques, traffic, etc.

Texts from related fields also should be part of the library. These include psychology, criminology, human relations, political science and others.

There are several periodicals which are worthwhile. By joining the International Association of Chiefs of Police the member is entitled to *The Police Chief*, a monthly publication. Most university police chiefs are eligible for membership in this organization either as associate or active members.

The Law Enforcement Bulletin, a monthly publication by the F.B.I., is available without cost upon request from the director.

There are several other publications available upon subscription.

Chapter IV

PERSONNEL ADMINISTRATION

E QUIPMENT, FACILITIES AND planning are of little consequence until personnel is added. Not until that point can the organization begin to function and move toward its intended goal. No matter how well equipped an organization may be, it will almost totally be dependent on its personnel for efficiency. The factors affecting the personnel of any organization must be arranged so that they enhance the efficiency, morale and integration of the unit. Consideration must be given to selection, training, advancement and general working conditions in order to achieve these goals.

BASIC QUALIFICATIONS FOR OFFICERS

Many, if not most, municipal police departments select officers under the regulations of a civil service board. While this is the case with some university police departments, it is not the rule. In June of 1969 a survey was conducted for the purpose of determining the personnel practices of university police departments. Only 22 percent of the eighty-six responding institutions reported that they were bound by civil service regulation regarding officer qualifications. This means that all the other institutions must provide their own criteria for choosing officers.

Each of the responding university police chiefs was asked to indicate the specific traits that he felt were important when considering a prospective university policeman. The respondents were asked to indicate their choices not their practices, as these often vary.

Age

Each university police chief was asked to indicate the age group from which he would prefer to hire recruits. He was given the choice of eighteen through twenty-three, the thirties and the forties.

One chief stated that he would like to hire eighteen-year-old recruits. Six chiefs chose age twenty-two, twelve chose twenty-three, sixty-two chose ages in the thirties, two chose the forties.

It was surprising to note the high number of chiefs who preferred officers in their thirties. I personally disagree with this choice after having hired and trained approximately 160 officers over an eight-year period.

I feel that by the time a man is in his thirties, he is set in many of his habits, both personal and professional. If he is that old when becoming a recruit he has obviously worked elsewhere. If he has worked as a law enforcement officer elsewhere he will have a series of habits that may not be compatible with the university police concept.

If the thirty-year-old recruit has not worked elsewhere in law enforcement, it may be cause for concern. Why is he desirous of changing occupation? Such a change could be indicative of an undesirable work history.

It is my contention that officers should be recruited early in life. They can then receive adequate training, and attitudes can be molded which will complement rather than clash with the academic community.

Physical Size

Most of the respondents chose to hire recruits of average size. None of them chose small men, and only a few chose large ones.

Here again I must part with the common choice. It has been my experience that the large man has less trouble in the field. They are required to deal with a clientele who are impressed with men of large physical stature. It has been my observation that most college-aged people, particularly men, are impressed by physical prowess. One need only to observe the status given the athlete on the campus.

I believe that it can be said that the larger officers are not so apt to have attacks against them as are those who are smaller. It has been my personal experience both as a field officer as well as a supervisor that the larger officers resort less often to physcial force than those smaller than the average.

I do not advocate sheer size as an advantage. I do, however, advocate well-exercised men with weight proportioned to height. At the Brigham Young University a program was instigated whereby each officer is required to meet a minimum physical fitness standard. Any officer who cannot qualify is placed on probation until such time that he can. If he shows no improvement after a reasonable time, he is asked to resign. During the probationary period he is not eligible for promotions or salary improvements.

The minimum requirements were determined with the assistance of the physical education department of the university. Very little resistance was met when they were instigated. It has resulted in only one dismissal, however, three men are currently on probation and have been notified of a deadline by which they must qualify.

Each man must be able to chin himself five times, do twenty-five situps, fifteen pushups and run a half mile in three minutes. The most difficulty has been experienced with the chinups. It is interesting to note that all who have failed to qualify are significantly overweight.

Undoubtedly all institutions of higher learning have physical fitness facilities available which can be scheduled for the use of the university police personnel. Consequently the excuse for not being fit because of the lack of equipment is generally not realistic.

When the program was initiated arrangements were made so that injuries sustained while engaged in approved physical fitness activities would be considered as occurring on duty for the purpose of medical benefits and sick leave.

Previous Police Experience

Sixty-seven percent of those polled in the survey indicated that they preferred applicants who had previous police experience. Twenty-three percent preferred that the applicant had no prior experience.

It is my preference to employ recruits with little or no experience. My personal experience with officers who have had extensive experience is that they are so set in their thinking that they seem to be constantly at odds with the university police concept. Their orientation is strongly that of enforcement with little concern for education and rehabilitation which in my opinion should be a facet of the university police officer's makeup.

I prefer to have officers with two or three years' experience. With that much service a new university police recruit will have a basic concept of general police practice, and may not be as rigid as officers who have had longer prior police service.

Education

Forty-two percent of the respondents indicated a preference for recruits with some college education. Thirty-four percent preferred to employ high-school graduates. Thirteen percent preferred college graduates. One chief indicated that he preferred recruits with only grade-school education.

Several university police departments have established a college degree as an entrance requirement. Wayne State University in Detroit not only requires a college degree, but the applicant must be accepted by graduate school and pursue an advanced degree.

The University of Utah requires an applicant for the police department to possess a four-year degree. It need not be in a field directly related to police work. It is felt that a university police officer will be more effective if he can adequately empathize with the students who are pursuing their studies as the officer formerly did. It is also felt that degree holding officers will receive more respect from the rest of the academic community.

While it is readily agreed that there is a dire need for more education among police officers, there is still some question as to whether or not college degrees should be required for recruits.

Many of the arguments against college educated police officers are made on an emotional plane by those who are police officers and do not have nor intend to obtain college degrees. The threat of college educated recruits to the high-school educated chief is obvious.

However, there are also some valid reasons for doubting the wisdom of requiring degrees from university police recruits.

It is agreed that those who have specialized or supervisory positions should have or be in the process of obtaining four-year degrees. However, I have some reservations about requiring a degree for new officers.

It is my opinion that very few officers enter police work with the aspiration of working as patrol officers. It is obvious that under our present system of policing that most of the personnel of the department will be assigned as such. Patrol work has a great deal of routine drudgery attached to it. While it is agreed that all officers should have some patrol experience, it is doubtful that most college graduates will be satisfied over a period of years to remain assigned to patrol. The goals of a college trained man are simply too high to keep him satisfied with the current concept of patrol work.

If college trained recruits are to be retained, the patrol function should be changed to provide added challenge. This can possibly be accomplished by eliminating detectives, and requiring the patrol officer to do the follow-up investigations rather than relying on special investigators.

Promotional procedure must be changed. In many instances the patrol officer must wait a number of years before he is eligible to take a promotional examination. If he is advanced he must then remain in that rank for a given period until he can take the examination for the next higher rank. Due to such procedures, officers of some municipal police departments must sometimes wait eleven years before they can compete for a captaincy, regardless of their competence.

The college educated officer may strongly feel that after three or four years experience he can handle a lieutenant's position without first being a sergeant. However, under present practices, he is not given an opportunity to try unless he has spent the required time as a sergeant. It is my opinion that such regulations stifle initiative and growth. I insist that if college educated officers are desirable, then the system must be altered to provide the challenge and growth that such men seek.

I prefer recruits who have one or two years' of college. They should be urged to continue their education while working. When they receive their degree it is very possible that they have the field experience necessary to qualify as supervisors or specialists. An officer with this background should be in a much stronger position to achieve a high grade on promotional examinations, which should be open to all members of the department, regardless of the time in rank. By following this procedure everyone has an equal opportunity for advancement.

THE SELECTION PROCESS

Surely everyone who has had the task of selecting personnel has longingly wished for some magic oracle through which they could be guided. The university police chief, bound by civil service regulations, has limited latitude in these matters. Those without civil service are faced with the problem of devising some procedure for selecting candidates best suited for the job.

A number of selection procedures are advocated. However, it is my contention, based on personal experience, that no single device is infallible. Personal judgment tempered with experience and a variety of tests seem to be the key. My contention is supported by O. Glen Stahl who states the following:

> . . . a single technique alone usually does not comprise a full examination. Nevertheless, the use of carefully validated and standardized techniques goes far to reduce the elements of change and caprice often present in the selection process. Where such devices are not employed, selection can be an uncertain matter indeed, for the man who can judge character and ability intuitively has been shown by psychological experiment to be nonexistent.[12]

The examinations traditionally administered for the purpose of selecting policemen are a written test, an oral interview, a physical agility test and a medical examination. In addition to these a background investigation is usually conducted. Some

---

[12] Stahl, O. Glenn: *Public Personnel Administration.* New York, Harper & Row, 1962, p. 72.

university police departments use all the above and in addition use an English test, a psychological test and a polygraph examination.

The composition of the oral board is of great importance. Representation from the following groups should be considered:

1. University police
2. Municipal police
3. University staff
4. Faculty
5. Student government

With this composition, at least one member being a female, the entire university community is represented.

At the conclusion of the interview, each board member rates the candidate, without consulting each other. Each candidate is rated with a numerical value on a scale from one to a hundred. The average rating is computed, and becomes the candidate's score.

The medical, physical agility and psychological tests are all fail-pass tests. Numerical scores are obtained on the written test, the English test and the oral interview.

For the purpose of administering and interpreting the psychological tests the university's testing and counselling center can be of aid. A personality test profile should be compiled on those recruits who are psychologically tested. Such a profile can be an aid when choosing officers again.

By adopting such procedures, many personnel problems can be lessened or eliminated.

In the survey, previously mentioned, it was reflected that almost all the university police departments use some form of oral test and background investigation. Approximately half of the eighty-six respondents use psychological tests and about one-fourth of the schools use polygraph screening.

As pointed out previously, there is no panacea to the problem of selecting personnel. However, there are some realistic procedures that can be employed with some degree of success.

TRAINING

Five percent of the university police departments responding to the survey indicated that they have no training program. Sixty-eight percent provide some sort of formalized in-service training. Forty-eight percent of the institutions send their police officers to a police academy for varying periods.

Fifty percent of the responding departments have appointed training officers. If a dynamic training program is desired, a training officer should be designated. He need not be of supervisory rank, but must possess the interest and ability to plan and execute training programs.

It is difficult to establish a training curriculum which pertains to all situations. The following list sets forth some basic police subjects:

Departmental organization
Rules and regulations of the department
Use of firearms
Care and use of equipment
Criminal law
City ordinances
Police records
Criminal investigation
Patrol methods
Sociology and criminology
Scientific aids
Physical fitness
First aid
Public disorders
Local and state geography
Psychology in police work
Public relations
Interrogation of suspects
Rules of evidence
Public speaking
Case preparation and court appearance[13]

[13] Clift, Raymond E.: *A Guide to Modern Police Thinking.* Cincinnati, The

W. H. Anderson Co., 1965, pp. 54-55.

In addition to the above subjects all departments should evaluate their own training needs and develop a program for meeting them.

The police executive must realize that training is a continuing process. It can never be said that the department is fully trained. After skills and concepts are learned they must constantly be reviewed and, at times, modified.

Training is expensive. Special appropriations must be provided in the police budget for this function. This should not only include funds for the actual training cost, but must also include cost for travel and overtime payments for officers who are forced to attend training when they normally would be off duty.

Training Programs and Aids

One of the most difficult problems for the training officer is that of developing materials for training. He can be much more effective if he keeps abreast of materials and programs produced by other agencies willing to share them.

Federal Bureau of Investigation Short Courses

The F.B.I. has assumed the responsibility of assisting state and local police officers with training. Regional short courses, on a variety of subjects are constantly being conducted. By contacting the local field office of the F.B.I., specific information can be obtained regarding attendance. By contacting the Special Agent in Charge of local field offices, it may be possible to have agents come to the campus and lecture to the university police officers.

State Training Programs

Many states maintain a state police academy. Several universities send their officers to such academies for training. Most states have funds obtained under the *Safe Streets and Omnibus Crime Bill* for the training of police officers. It may be possible, depending on the official attitudes of the various state governments, for university officers to attend the police academy without cost to the university.

The Training Key

The International Association of Chiefs of Police has a training service available to departments whose heads are members of the association. *The Training Key* is a publication sent monthly to the participating department. It costs two dollars annually per officer. Subjects of wide police interests are treated. Each Key has a material outline, as well as an instructor's outline. An excellent bibliography and examination questions are also included.

Local Seminars

Most university police departments experience a lull during the summer. This is a luxury which the training officer should capitalize on. He should prepare to present several short seminars. They can be planned in cooperation with the local police. There are some real advantages in training university and municipal officers together.

With the current likelihood of civil disruptions university and municipal police officers trained together are more likely to function as a unit. In many instances, it is impossible for the university police to handle disturbances without outside police assistance. A certain loyalty between the groups may develop which is advantageous. The desirability of uniform procedure during such incidents is obvious and needs no further mention.

PROMOTIONS

As promotional opportunities arise, the police executive may be faced with the same basic problem he faced when recruiting new officers. The issue, of course, is who should be promoted?

Again, those who are bound by civil service regulations may have little choice in the matter, but others may have a serious morale problem brewing.

The procedure should probably follow the same general course as outlined for screening recruits. Those to be considered for promotion should be given a series of tests with the objective of choosing the man best suited for the position.

Some difficulty lies in identifying those eligible to take the examination. Basic questions must be answered. Can only sergeants take the lieutenants' examination? Can only patrolmen with three years' experience take the investigator examination? These questions were alluded to in the preceding section dealing with college graduate recruits.

Having structured several promotional examinations, I have experienced fewer problems when they have been open to all officers of the department. When this procdure is followed, the test must be carefully constructed to specifically measure the traits necessary to the position in question.

By making the test open to all, everyone feels that he has an opportunity for advancement. The old timer also realizes that he is not going to be promoted through mere longevity. In order to achieve, candidates will have to be prepared to successfully compete for advancements.

If an open examination is to be administered, it is essential to obtain concensus from those affected, prior to its implementation. There may be those who feel that they are heirs to certain positions. They may feel that an open examination is specially designed to pass them over. It must be clearly pointed out that they have the same opportunity as others. They should understand that their prior experience will give them a greater chance for achieving on the tests.

It may be advisable to compute seniority to the overall examination score. The candidate with longevity is then given an advantage that he may be entitled to. This can easily be accomplished by allowing a certain number of points for a given unit of time.

Chapter V

RECORDS AND REPORTS

Rᴇɢᴀʀᴅʟᴇss ᴏғ ᴛʜᴇ type or size of university police departments, one commodity that should not be omitted is records. Some campuses are policed without guns, cars, investigators and a number of other things, but not without records. Admittedly some of the records systems employed are primitive, but even then they do exist, although in rudimentary form.

The record system becomes, in effect, the memory of the department. If it is indexed effectively, one can find facts that have long been forgotten. It becomes the yardstick of performance. By evaluating the data contained therein it can be determined if the objectives of the organization are being met. If they are not, a careful perusal of the records may indicate why.

Records may act as a barometer, predicting future needs. The astute police chief will watch the trends reflected in his records. By daily field report evaluation, he can initiate or alter his procedural, tactical and operational plans.

Reports from the field may indicate a need for immediate action. In this way records act as a thermometer, signalling hot areas needing swift response. This should trigger selective enforcement, surveillance or saturation of patrol or other field action until the reports indicate a cooling effect.

Good records are essential to good decision making. The policies of any organization are dynamic and will need constant modification. New and improved methods must be found to supplant those found to be ineffective. The constant evaluation of records may signal a need for improvement. Etzioni, commenting on the decision-making theories of March and Simon states the following:

> . . . organizations seek a *satisfying* solution rather than an optimum one. This means that search behavior will be stopped once

a pattern is found which is considered reasonably good, acceptable. A new search will be triggered when organizational performance falls below that level.[14]

It would appear in the best interest of the organization to have the search triggered as soon as possible. The trigger mechanism can be a number of things. For a policing agency it can be the clamor from the public, the acid editorials, physical attack on officers and others. It would be much better to have the record system, along with inspections, be the mechanism triggering change.

There are many reports which comprise the typical police record system. The most typical ones will be discussed.

COMPLAINT REPORT

This report has many names. It is known as a "crime report," "incident report," "trouble report" and undoubtedly others. Regardless of name the function is essentially the same, and will hereafter be called a complaint report. It is the spine of the record system, and is the basic report to which almost all other reports refer.

A complaint report should be written whenever an incident arises which requires police action. It should also be written when an incident is significant enough to be made a matter of record, even if no police action beyond making a report is necessary.

Many of the incidents brought to the attention of the university police are so minor that a written report may seem superfluous, and sometimes a log entry only is sufficient. It is very difficult to establish a policy dictating when a report is required. An incident may initially seem insignificant and then later become extremely important. The field officer's competence, augmented by a field supervisor's experience, will usually dictate the policy as each incident arises.

All complaint reports must be completed before the reporting officer finishes his shift.. They should then be given perusal by a

---

[14] Etzioni, Amitai: *Modern Organizations.* Englewood Cliffs, New Jersey, Prentice-Hall, Inc., 1964, p. 31.

supervisor who will also determine if any follow-up investigation is needed.

ARREST REPORT

The arrest report is used for the purpose of recording the pertinent facts regarding the physical arrest of a suspect. It should describe the events leading to the arrest, what violation of law was observed, how was the probable cause established for the arrest? It should describe the steps taken in making the arrest, particularly if physical force was necessary. Utterances of a voluntary unsolicited nature made by the arrestee should be recorded. The arresting officer must include in the report that he advised the suspect of his civil rights before questioning commenced. Circumstances surrounding searches and seizures of evidence must be recounted in detail.

The arrest report and the complaint report should not work to the exclusion of each other; rather, they complement each other. A complaint report may exist without an arrest report; the reverse should never be the case.

A complaint report may be received by the police wherein it is reported that a person's car stereo has been stolen. Subsequent complaint reports may be received describing a similar incident. Due to the high frequency of thefts a stake-out is initiated. When a suspect is observed taking a car stereo, he is arrested. Subsequently he admits to several other thefts, which have been reported on earlier complaint reports. At this time an arrest report is completed. It describes the incident of the arrest, and refers to the other complaint reports, One arrest report then exists with several related crimes reported on separate complaint reports.

For statistical purposes it is advantageous to have the two separate reports. The arrest reports will reflect the number of arrests, the complaint reports the number of reported crimes.

IDENTIFICATION RECORD

The most common form of identification record is probably the fingerprint card. It bears the fingerprints of an individual, in addition to his physical description address, occupation, scars, tattoos, aliases, signature and photograph.

The fingerprint card is an excellent record for identification purposes. However, it is completed only when an arrest is made. Many cases handled by the university police do not involve arrest and prosecution, but are referred to the university disciplinary system for disposition. Many, if not most, of these students have been involved in misconduct amounting to a crime, but are not charged. Unless some provision is made for fingerprinting and photographing these individuals, no substantial identification record will exist in the university police files for use in subsequent investigations.

Approximately seven years ago the Brigham Young University police initiated a program whereby all offenders of the law were fingerprinted and photographed. This included those students who were not prosecuted as well as those who were. This procedure has proven beneficial in several ways.

The person who is fingerprinted and photographed has a feeling that he has been caught. All feelings of anonymity are removed. He knows that he is known and is on record with the police. The likelihood of his being apprehended again if he commits a subsequent offense is possibly enhanced. This may be a factor toward eliminating his desire to violate the law again.

The information in the identification file gives an investigator a great reservoir of data which aids him immensely. Several cases have been solved directly through this source, both from the comparison of fingerprints and other data found on the fingerprint card.

This program was not initiated for the purpose of giving the student a criminal record in the general sense. It is merely a record kept by the university police until the student leaves the university, after which it is destroyed by burning. If the student was prosecuted, the record remains as in the case of any citizen who is prosecuted.

The card used in the case where no prosecution is initiated is a different size than the regular eight by eight inch fingerprint card. This precaution is taken to avoid its being sent to some permanent state or federal fingerprint file. Even if the card should accidently be sent, it would not be accepted because of its odd size.

When a student is apprehended, but not charged, he is informed that the taking of his fingerprints will not give him a criminal record. He is assured that they are for the university's use only, and that they will be destroyed after he graduates. In the case of a student being charged criminally, a set of prints are sent to the state bureau of identification, as prescribed by law, and to the Federal Bureau of Investigation. These records become a permanent part of the individual's criminal history and will be removed only upon an expungement order of a competent court.

PROPERTY REPORT

Police work inevitably involves the seizure of property belonging to others. It must be cared and accounted for at all times. The property may be contraband, evidence or lost property turned over to the police. Frequently, the police will have to take charge of property belonging to arrestees, the injured, the dead, or people otherwise unable to care for their personal property.

To adequately account for all property in police custody a property report should be used. It must be designed to serve both as an account record as well as a receipt at the time of seizure.

A property report must contain a detailed description of the seized property. All distinguishing features must be specifically described. Any damage existing at the time of seizure should be carefully noted in the report. The report must indicate where the property is stored so that it can easily be found upon demand. Space must be provided for the signatures of those to whom the property is released from police custody.

MISCELLANEOUS REPORTS

The specific reports and records mentioned in the preceding pages are basic to any police operation. There are several other reports that are of great help, but may not be applicable to every department.

Officers' Daily Log

The purpose of this report is to give the field officer an opportunity to record the events of his tour of duty. If designed carefully, this report can be a very valuable management tool. It reflects units of work accomplished by the officer in relationship to the time spent in the field. It makes it possible for the chief to account for the time expended on various field functions. He can show that for a given number of patrol miles or hours the department recovered a certain amount of property, made so many arrests and wrote a certain number of citations. He can show that the officers' time was spent on answering calls; hence there was no preventive patrol during certain high-frequency crime hours. These points may indicate a need for additional patrol officers or cars.

Field Interview Cards

The adoption of a field interview card system gives the department an excellent preventive and investigative tool. The card is used for the purpose of recording the identity of individuals observed at unusual hours in unusual places under unusual circumstances. Not only does it become a valuable record for subsequent use, but the officer's contact with the citizen in the field can have a salutary effect.

The card, completed by the patrol officer, should be supplemented with several cross-indexes. Those commonly used are day, time, location, car driven and companions.

The following example illustrates the value of the field interview card to an investigation.

At 2:30 A.M. an officer observes a vehicle being driven slowly across the campus. The driver is a young man with another young male passenger. The vehicle bears no university parking permit, or other evidence of belonging on campus. The officer stops the vehicle and asks the driver and passenger for identification. It is determined that they are local residents claiming to be on their way home from a late party. The officer completes a field interview card on both subjects after which he resumes his patrol activities.

Two days later a student telephoned that his car stereo has

been stolen. He had not intended to report it, but his insurance company will not settle without a police report being filed. As a matter of routine, the victim is asked for the time when he last knew his stereo was in his car. He states that it was taken two days ago and that he knew it was in the car when he parked it at 1:00 A.M.

An investigator is assigned to the case. He goes to the field interview time-file and pulls the cards indexed to interviews conducted after 12:30 A.M. on the date of the theft. He also checks the location and date file corresponding to the theft he is investigating. He soon discovers that the two interview cards completed by the patrol officer several nights before have the names of two good suspects.

He arranges an interview with the suspects and consequently recovers the stereo reported stolen on the night of the field interview, and several others as well.

The foregoing case is not at all remote. Several incidents are known where the solution to a crime was found because an alert patrol officer had conducted a field interview, and made a record of it.

Many of the people interviewed in the field will be citizens on legitimate business. It is imperative that the officers be well trained in the procedures of field interviewing. If training is neglected, it is possible that the effects of a sound program will be negated by the poor approach of an officer. A citizen who has been interviewed should leave with the feeling that the university police is doing a good job in a courteous manner.

Traffic Related Reports

A large percentage of the university police activities deal with matters relating to traffic. This important function will require several special report forms.

Some of the most common ones are citations, traffic accident reports and forms necessary for the registering of cars on the campus.

Citations

A citation form must be printed for issuance when a parking or moving violation is observed. There are an unbelievable variety of citation forms in use. It is probably advantageous to have a separate form for moving and parking citations, as the information needed on each is different.

The form must provide a place to write the identity of the violator, the time and location of the vehicle and specifically how the law was violated.

Traffic Accident Reports

Forms must be provided so that field officers can properly record the results of traffic accident investigations.

The liability of parties to a traffic accident may eventually have to be established in court. The investigating officer may be called to testify to his findings at the scene of the accident. With the court calendars as crowded as they now are, it may take two or three years before a civil trial will be held. Unless the officer thoroughly investigated and recorded the results of the investigation, he cannot adequately serve the involved parties. A good traffic accident report can often determine whether or not the injured party will receive a just settlement.

Thorough and complete traffic accident reports may reflect traffic engineering problems. The reports should be reviewed regularly to determine if engineering defects are contributing to accidents.

Traffic accident reports will also indicate a need for added or special enforcement. The primary cause of accidents should be determined. Once identified it should be examined to see if special enforcement directed at a particular violation could reduce the likelihood of recurrent accidents.

Forms for the following purposes should be made available for traffic accident reporting.

1. Reporting statements of parties and witnesses.
2. Reporting the officer's findings at the scene.
3. Reporting the personal data concerning parties and witnesses.
4. Recording the result of field sobriety tests.
5. Computing and recording wheel skid tests.

The forms should be prepared in such a way that they are of value to the involved parties and their insurance companies.

Vehicle Registration Forms

Almost all universities have several forms relating to the task of registering motor vehicles and bicycles. These vary so greatly that little can be said here about what is best. The forms will have to be designed to fit the objective of the individual parking system. Most chiefs are gracious in sharing their forms for mutual betterment. The informaticn gleaned from this source can be very helpful in designing similar programs.

Referral Reports

This type of report may have many names. Its purpose is to refer a matter to the disciplinary system of the university.

After the police has concluded its investigation, the results must be recorded. A report must be written so that those responsible for the disposition of the matter will have all available information.

The complaint report is not sufficient for this purpose. It does not reflect the information needed by the dean's office. The referral should describe the violation of law or university regulation. A brief outline of the investigative procedure should be included. The interaction between the officer and the student should be related in some detail, as this will often reflect a great deal regarding the general attitude of the violator.

The reporting officer should, of course, avoid any emotional reporting as this might be detrimental to the student.

The Central Index Card

For records to be used as a tool there must be a simple way of retrieving information. In that most do not have sophisticated data processing equipment available a more simple procedure must be devised.

The central index becomes the key to the entire records system. It contains cards that are filed in alphabetical order using the last name of the person mentioned in the report to which the card is indexed. It is helpful to type all last names in capital letters in any report. This procedure tends to minimize filing errors.

Each report should have a separate file number. One of the copies must be filed numerically. The report number, as well as other data, is typed on the card. Each person mentioned by name in the report will have a card in the file with the number of the report on it. By checking the central index file it becomes a simple task to determine if a person has been mentioned in connection with any report.

If an individual is mentioned in more than one report only one index card is completed, but it will bear all the relevant report numbers. When a report is received it becomes necessary to search the index file to see if the persons named in it already have index cards. If they do the new report number is merely added to the existing card.

Only one person should be assigned the responsibility of refiling index cards that have been removed from the file.

Many universities have computers on the campus. The police chief should investigate the possibility of utilizing this service. Ideally the police department should have a computer terminal by its communications center. Data can then be readily available without a manual search of files. The future possibility of using computers for records storage should be kept in mind when designing any record system. It is wise to consult with a computer expert when designing a conventional record system so that a future adaptation to computer service can be accomplished with little difficulty.

Chapter VI

COMMUNITY RELATIONS

Recently the subject of police-community relations has received a great deal of attention. This has been a healthy phenomenon and should be encouraged on the university campus as well as in the municipality.

The university police probably have to deal with the most vocal and critical public anywhere. It seems that university students, as well as other members of the academic community, are impatient with anything short of perfection.

To do an adequate job the university police must initiate programs designed to engender support from those who are to be served. The initiative rests with the police. It is the duty of the university police executive to plan and execute programs for soliciting public support for the university law enforcement unit.

Community relations programs should be taken to the people of the surrounding community as well as to those affiliated directly with the university. University law enforcement activity needs support from the citizens of the municipality as well as from the academic community.

SPEAKERS PROGRAM

One of the best means of obtaining general support is possibly through public speaking. The many social and service groups within the university provide a natural forum. By developing the ability of certain officers to speak publicly, this can be a very rewarding progarm.

Frequently the success of the speakers program lies not so much in what is discussed, but rather how it is presented and the image the officer exhibits to the audience. It is important for the students to perceive the officers as intelligent, articulate men with warmth and a sincere interest in others.

There are several topics that are of current interest to students and others. The university police should select several and prepare presentations on them. Then if an invitation is extended the department can respond.

The chief should always stand ready to speak to any group. He should be prepared to candidly answer questions about all facets of his operational responsibility.

Campus housing units are especially fertile for speaking. A very informative and tasteful presentation can be taken to the girls' residence halls to discuss matters relating to personal safety and the prevention of sex crimes.

Many off-campus groups are interested in subjects that the university police officer can treat. The Chamber of Commerce will be happy to hear what the university police can do when students write bad checks, shoplift or fail to pay debts. Topics relating to drug abuse are very popular with most groups. The list of topics is limited only by lack of imagination, but should be chosen so that the presentation is tasteful and does not reveal confidential material.

SPECIAL COURSES

There are a number of special courses that the university police can conduct for the benefit of the university community. Such topics as self-defense for women, first aid, driver improvement and gun safety are a few that might be appropriate. I have personally conducted several classes in self-defense for women, and it was found to be a very effective public relations tool.

MISCELLANEOUS PROGRAMS

There are several programs that are worthwhile and can be easily implemented.

Student Group Adviser

Many universities require student groups to have faculty advisers or sponsors. There is little reason why university police officers cannot function in this capacity. This involves the officer with the students in a nonpolice role which will have a positive effect on both the officer and students. Officers have served as advisers to sportscar clubs, alpine clubs, law enforcement clubs and to a few fraternal organizations.

Open House

If adequate facilities are available it may be possible to have an open house. Equipment and artifacts may be displayed in a way to generate interest. Law week or law observance week could be opportune times for such an activity.

At certain times during the year it may be possible for the university police to sponsor speakers who could treat subjects relative to law observance and support of law enforcement.

Speedometer Check

An announcement can be made in the university paper that on a given date the police will make its traffic radar available for citizens to check the accuracy of their speedometers.

Marking Personal Property

The public can be urged to come to a predetermined location at which the police will mark theft-prone property for future identification. Such property as car stereos, hub caps, etc., would be particularly appropriate.

Fingerprinting

Many students need fingerprints for a variety of reasons. Some agencies require fingerprints before students can be employed. The university police should have the facilities for rendering this type of service.

Research Resources

Students constantly need assistance with term projects or other research work. The university police should keep materials available dealing with current problems. Students can then come to the police and obtain assistance with their projects. By being cordial and genuinely interested the police may get the reputation of being friends rather than foes.

Classroom Appearances

The faculty should be made aware that members of the university police are available for classroom appearances. Officers who are particularly capable of communicating well should be selected to fill any appointments of this nature. Such activities can be very fruitful for the officer, as well as students.

The Individual Officer

No matter how many community relations programs are initiated, the individual officer is the most important key to a successful effort.

Every field contact he makes is a community relations opportunity. A serious effort must be made to instill in each officer the attitudes that will place the department in a favorable light. Only officers who have the ability and the desire to be true public servants should be employed by the university police.

The very appearance and demeanor of the officer will radiate a certain image. Every effort must be made to make it a favorable one.

BIBLIOGRAPHY

Clift, Raymond E.: *A Guide to Modern Police Thinking.* Cincinnati, The W. H. Anderson Company, 1965.

Etzioni, Amitai: *Modern Organizations.* Englewood Cliffs, N. J., Prentice-Hall, Inc., 1964.

Gourley, G. Douglas, and Bristow, Allen P.: *Patrol Administration.* Springfield, Ill., Charles C Thomas, 1966.

International City Managers' Association: *Municipal Police Administration.* Chicago, International City Managers' Association, 1954.

Jones, Leland V.: *Scientific Investigation and Physical Evidence.* Springfield, Ill., Charles C Thomas, 1959.

Koga, Robert K., and Nelson, John G.: *The Koga Method: Police Baton Technique.* Beverly Hills, Calif., The Glencoe Press, 1968.

Nedrud, Duane R.: *The Criminal Law 1968.* Chicago, L. E. Publishers, 1968.

Nevin, David: Charlie Whitman: The Eagle Scout Who Grew Up With A Tortured Mind. *Life,* August, 1966, pp. 28-29.

Pfiffner, John M., and Sherwood, Frank P.: *Administrative Organization.* Englewood Cliffs, N. J., Prentice-Hall, Inc., 1966.

Stahl, O. Glenn: *Public Personnel Administration.* New York, Harper & Row, Publishers, 1962.